Landscapes of Participatory Making, Modding and Hacking

Landscapes of Participatory Making, Modding and Hacking:

Maker Culture and Makerspaces

Edited by

Kenneth Y T Lim

Cambridge
Scholars
Publishing

Landscapes of Participatory Making, Modding and Hacking:
Maker Culture and Makerspaces

Edited by Kenneth Y T Lim

This book first published 2017

Cambridge Scholars Publishing

Lady Stephenson Library, Newcastle upon Tyne, NE6 2PA, UK

British Library Cataloguing in Publication Data
A catalogue record for this book is available from the British Library

ISBN (10): 1-4438-5066-7
ISBN (13): 978-1-4438-5066-7

TABLE OF CONTENTS

LIST OF TABLES AND FIGURES

PREFACE

The impetus to write this book came in the summer of 2014, when some of the authors represented within these pages had just participated in a lively panel discussion during the annual conference of the Royal Geographical Society that year.

Entitled *Geographies of making: the jazz of participatory fabrication, improvisation and hackerspaces*, its Call for Proposals read as follows:

> The Industrial Revolution of the nineteenth century introduced the world to mass production and to Fordist production flows. In the late twentieth century, phenomena such as jet travel, the internet, and outsourcing prompted some pundits (eg, Friedman, 2005) to propose metaphors of a flattened world, with concomitant implications on space, geography and the (supposed) death of distance.
>
> As our present century unfolds, technologies and socio-cultural phenomena such as the internet of things, crowd-sourcing, digital fabrication, and wearable computing are not only democratizing the potentialities of participatory design, prototyping and production, but are also becoming increasingly enmeshed with – and breathing new life into – ways of making more associated with cottage industries than with how production has been studied and understood for at least the past hundred years.
>
> As circuits mashup with woodcraft and beadwork, as the clothes we wear identify themselves with their own unique digital signatures, and as interest-groups carve out fabricative spaces of their own across major urban centres worldwide, what might the implications to all we have studied and known about the geographies of industrialization, of industrial location, of urbanization, of regional divides be? What might some of the narratives be behind the emergence of maker cultures and hackerspaces?

This call is still relevant today. These pages represent an assemblage of such stories, and it is hoped you will draw your inspiration from them, as you seek to chart your own journey in the making.

The chapters in the remainder of this book develop these preceding themes in a myriad of ways.

Reference

Friedman, T. L. 2005. *The world is flat: a brief history of the 21st century.* New York: Farrar, Straus, and Giroux.

Chapter One

Doorways to Making

Kenneth Y T Lim

In January 2013, a new school year was beginning in Singapore. My team of research assistants and I were at a state-funded school, helping a geography teacher with her lesson, using an immersive environment that we had co-designed. I was heartened to see the Grade Ten students in animated conversation during the discussion, until I realised that what they were so excitedly talking about was not their experiences from the lesson.

Instead, I found them sharing pictures from their phones. I squinted to try to make out what the pictures were depicting, but I could not. Have a go at making this one out:

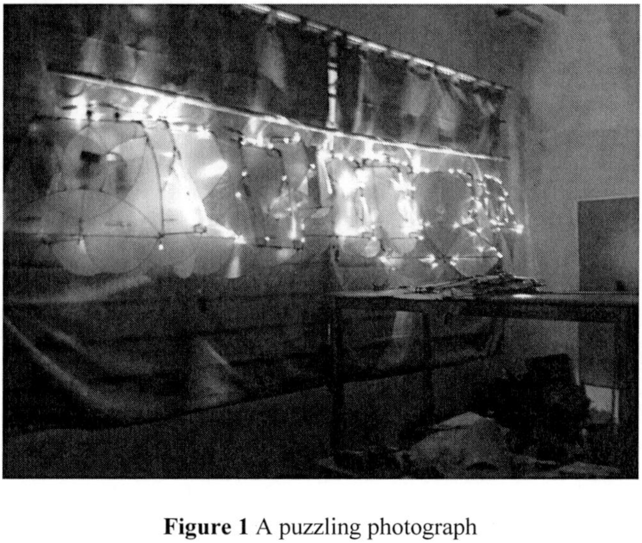

Figure 1 A puzzling photograph

It turned out that this was a photograph of radio-controlled kites.

The students were very excited about this and similar photographs because they had spent the better part of their December holidays modifying / "modding" / "hacking" these kites with light-emitting diodes (LEDs) and trying to improve their flying characteristics. The students were showing a lot more interest in sharing these photographs than in discussing their experiences of our carefully designed formal curriculum lesson.

It turns out that there was a fascinating story behind this simple photograph, which – at first glance – shows something quite unintelligible.

And therein lies a metaphor, which runs throughout the chapters in this book. Namely, attempting to describe the landscapes of making, maker culture, and makerspaces is an endeavour which requires intentionality and keen observation while rewarding patience and respect. And one never knows when Schrödinger's Cat might show up.

As serendipity would have it, January 2013 marked my introduction to maker culture and makerspaces in a fairly elaborate way for even before the aforementioned geography lesson, I was fortunate enough to spend a week in early January visiting makerspaces on both the East and West Coasts of the United States. If I learned anything from these visits, it was that cultures of making dialectically evolve from their respective local socio-cultures. Since that first visit, I have also had the privilege of visiting makerspaces in East Asia, such as in Hong Kong and Singapore. Whether it be Dim Sum Labs or HackManhattan, Noisebridge or hackerspace.sg, a great many cultures of making still – for better or worse – situate themselves along the periphery of (what might loosely be constituted as) the "mainstream"; in fact, such peripheries are not only metaphorical but quite literal in terms of their siting within urban morphologies.

Closely coupled with such peripheral situations is the question of access. It is not uncommon for makerspaces to not only situate themselves behind closed doors but behind such doors with elaborate – and sometimes deliberately obfuscated – protocols of access. Take, for example, the following figure.

Figure 2 A closed unmarked door

This innocuous unmarked door in a school in Singapore represents the sole means of access to the magic of the student-initiated makerspace described later in this chapter. One can imagine how easy it is to walk past it. In fact, that is precisely what adults are supposed to do; on the obverse of this door, inside the actual space, one finds this sign:

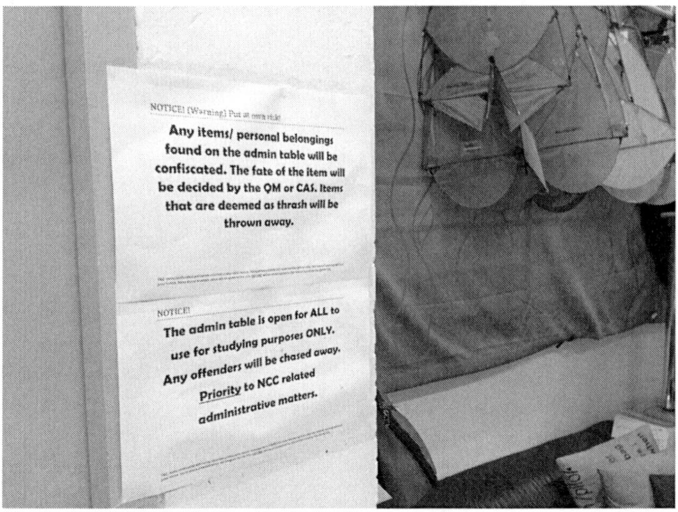

Figure 3 Access protocols

Across the landscapes of making, such issues of periphery and access are more common than one would think. Thus, for example, we have the façade of Noisebridge in San Francisco:

Figure 4 Noisebridge

And the façade of Dim Sum Labs in Hong Kong:

Figure 5 Dim Sum Labs

It can therefore be seen that from their origins in the polytechnic and vocational cultures of Germany, makerspaces have crossed oceans and emerged and /or attempted to be nurtured in countries such as South Korea, Thailand and Singapore (Endgadget, 2004). The story of the students and their modded kites transcends the boundaries of both the formal and non-formal curricula. Specifically, schools in Singapore oblige students to participate in at least one so-called co-curricular activity (CCA). The CCAs organize after-school activities with the aim of building character and leadership qualities among the students.

One example of a uniformed CCA group is the National Cadet Corps (Air) (NCC (Air)). The NCC (Air) curriculum has two main components: foot drills and aeromodelling. To build a healthy sense of competition and *esprit de corps* across the various NCC (Air) units placed in schools in Singapore, annual aeromodelling competitions are organized on an inter-school basis.

A corollary of the training as student-cadets prepare for such tournaments is that their remote-controlled scale-model aircraft will crash and will need to be repaired or replaced. Each school-based NCC (Air) unit is given autonomy with regards to crafting the curricular enactments in order to best prepare the cadets to fly the aircraft skillfully. At the school described in this study, the NCC (Air) student-cadets designed a scaffolded curriculum spanning the four years of secondary school. The novice trainees (typically aged twelve to thirteen) are introduced to the principles and concepts of flight through flight simulation software (see Figure 6). They then progress to practicing on remote-controlled powered-kites, and finally to the scale-model aircraft.

Figure 6 Novice trainees practising on a flight simulator

What distinguished the student-cadets at the school from their counterparts at other schools in Singapore is that they had developed a strong "can do" / improvisational spirit within themselves, and this was primarily evident in how they approached tinkering with and repairing the design of the stock, off-the-shelf kites and model aircraft they flew (see Figure 7).

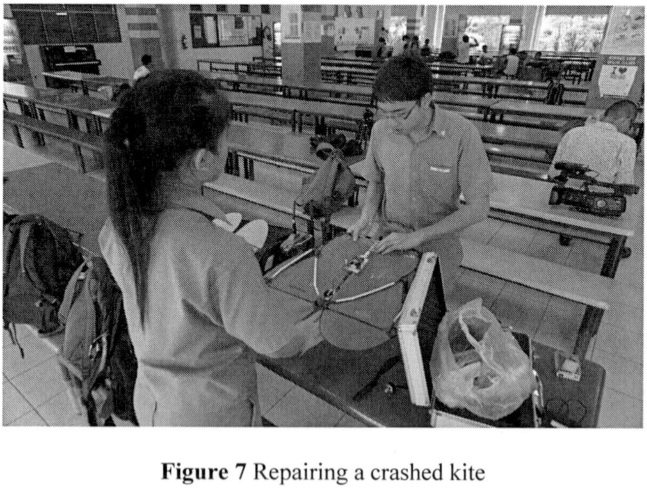

Figure 7 Repairing a crashed kite

Of equal interest is how some of the more senior student-members within the team went beyond just tinkering with the design of flying models, and cannibalized parts to diversify into land-based (Figure 8), and even prototype water-based, craft.

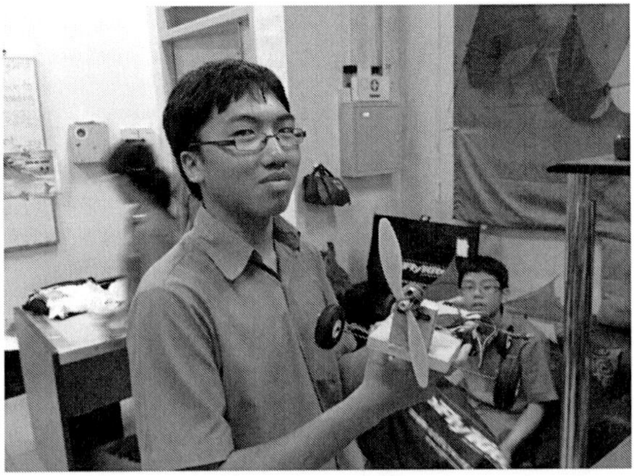

Figure 8 Cannibalisation of aeromodelling parts to craft a land-based go-kart

To elaborate, six of the senior student-members began to iterate designs and prototypes. A blueprint for an early design is shown in Figure 9.

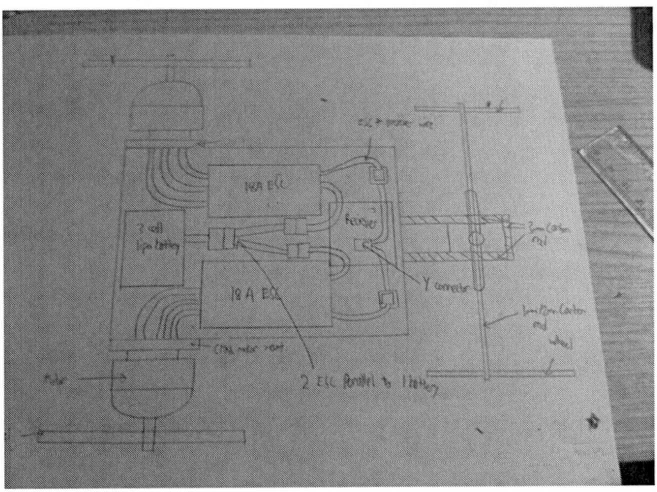

Figure 9 An early blueprint for the Improvised go-kart

In focus group discussions with the students, they described this initial design as follows:

> The RC Car V1's body was to have been made of wood. The car would have been propelled forward by the two motors driving its back wheels. The rotation of the wheels would depend on the plastic servo located at the front of the car. However, the RC Car V1 was not built as there were various safety concerns and budget issues.

The number of bespoke parts needed for their first iteration led them to look for possible sources to cannibalise. They described their thinking thus:

> The RC Car V2 was conceptualised and subsequently built but there is no image available as it was dismantled on the same day it was constructed. The car's body was made of wood. The car was made with two sets of Cessna (aircraft) landing gear. It was intended to showcase how Cessna parts could be readapted to serve a different function as a demonstration of creativity. One of the landing gear was glued at the back of the car while the other landing gear was attached to a servo, allowing the car to turn. A motor was attached to the back of the car in order to propel the car forward.

The students shared that during the course of their iterative attempts, they appropriated – with the permission and supervision of teachers – parts, materials and machining tools from the school's metalworking workshop managed by the Design and Technology Department, even though they were not necessarily taking Design and Technology as an academic subject.

In fact, they went even further, because in some cases they found the soldering tools "not precise enough". In these cases, they leveraged their social capital with the proprietor of the local kite-supplier to gain access to the better-maintained and up-to-date tools found in the proprietor's personal workshop, even though this entailed a half-hour bus journey beyond their local estate.

Of particular interest was that – as they continued iterating the design, and because they were personally invested in a task which was both authentic and meaningful – the student-cadets gradually appropriated the epistemic frame (Shaffer, 2007) of the designer and the engineer; thus, for example, they were able to describe a subsequent iteration of the go-kart (Figure 10):

The RC Car V3 reuses the same wooden car body used by RC Car V2. However, a major design alteration involves wheels connected by carbon rods instead of the Cessna landing gear. This alteration was made to lower the centre of gravity so that the car would be more stable. A Karbonite servo was used to turn the wheels instead of a plastic servo as the plastic servo will vibrate the moment the wheels are attached.

Figure 10 Refined chassis with a low centre of gravity

In these and other ways, the maker culture that has spontaneously emerged within the NCC (Air) at the school found enactions through seamlessly negotiating formal and non-formal structures of time and space within and without the schooling curriculum of an East Asian society more often associated with rules, laws, fines and regimented prescription.

To summarise, learners engaging in participatory performances in which they derive authenticity thrive on – and look forward to – having their respective creative processes critiqued by social others; one only needs to look at trust-based online communities – such as Flickr, YouTube, eBay, Amazon and fan-authored wikis – for evidence of this. This can be thought of as akin to a shift from a quasi-Cartesian "I am what I own / I am what I control" to "I am what I share with others to build upon".

For example, Figure 11 shows a more stereotypical conception of what might be expected from a uniformed CCA group, and is all the more remarkable because it depicts the same student-cadets (on parade) as those who are active participants in their local makerspace.

Figure 11 Makers on parade

This case example suggests that the student-cadets were successfully able to negotiate formalized regimental protocols as well as leverage – often informally through their own social networks – seemingly peripheral actors and structures such as kite-sellers, metal-working workshops and tools. They were able to operate fluently across what might initially come across as hard boundaries because they derived meaning and authenticity from their membership and participation in interest-driven communities. No one needed to tell them to persevere and improve; instead, they engaged in a complex series of performances encompassing goal-setting, resource evaluation and self- and peer-assessment according to both personal and socially moderated standards.

Fabricated using funds initially pooled from their own savings, and using scrap materials and tools from the metal- and woodworking workshop in the school, the go-karts and subsequent craft represent authentic examples of remix and *thinkering* that reflect the kinds of students East Asian societies will have to increasingly depend upon in order to stay relevant, adaptive and responsive in the 21st century. Going forward, it would do well for state-funded initiatives to consider how passion-driven street-craft communities might be encouraged through the provision of infrastructure, and access to shared resources, tools and expertise. The role that schools could potentially play in this process – in more structured ways – is taken up in the next chapter.

References

Engadget. (2004) “Shanghai Science and Technology Commission Proposes 100 'Innovation Houses' for DIYers”. Retrieved February 14, 2013 from http://www.engadget.com/2011/11/12/shanghai-science-and-technology-commission-proposes-100-innovat/

Shaffer, D. W. (2007) *How Computer Games Help Children Learn*. New York: Palgrave.

CHAPTER TWO

ESTABLISHING A FABLAB IN A SCHOOL

SUSAN JUST

In the preceding chapter, a case study was shared on how a makerspace spontaneously emerged from within a co-curricular activity in a school in Singapore. This chapter focuses on how attempts to nurture such maker dispositions in a more intentional manner have resulted in a success story in a school in the Australian state of Victoria.

Lauriston Girls' School is an independent non-denominational girls' school founded in 1901. It has an enrolment of approximately 1000 students, spread between Kindergarten, Junior School and Senior School. The school is co-educational in the Kindergarten, three- and four-year-old classes, and all girls from Prep to Year 12.

Students from the Lauriston Girls' School meet peers from a wide range of cultures. Their families exemplify life and work in a global community. Lauriston families come from a range of ethnic backgrounds which include students from China, Singapore, New Zealand, Malaysia, the United Kingdom and the United States of America.

Year 9 Lauriston students attend a rural campus – Howqua – which is situated near the township of Mansfield, approximately three hours from Melbourne. Attending school from Monday to Sunday, the students complete their academic curriculum and an outdoor programme, which is run two days of each week. The students undertake the programme in five-week blocks and return to their families in Melbourne for an exeat at the conclusion of each five-week block.

The Howqua campus was established on 250 hectares of bushland, and includes classroom facilities, a dining hall and kitchen, a library, art and music rooms, a performing arts building and nine Houses for students.

Lauriston Girls' School is a non-selective school. Both the Victorian Certificate of Education (VCE) and the International Baccalaureate Diploma programmes are offered in Years 11 and 12. Most students enter into a tertiary course of study. Students choose a broad variety of tertiary courses, including Arts, Science, Medicine, Bio-medicine, Engineering, Architectural Design, Visual Arts, Design, and Marketing and Communications.

The vision, mission and values of Lauriston Girls' School

At the heart of the Lauriston Girls' School is a vision for girls' education that encompasses pedagogical, environmental and pastoral considerations. Central to the success of this vision is the ability of the school staff to think beyond the "now" to plan for an ever-changing and complex future.

Vision: The school for life.
Mission: It is our mission to enhance the lifelong learning capabilities of all students.
Values: The values of the school are:

1. **Relationships:**
   The most effective learning occurs when the teacher / learner relationship is well established. Developing tolerant relationships irrespective of status, race or culture is a fundamental life skill.
2. **Courage:**
   Developing the courage to ask, act independently, think differently, face physical and moral challenges and make decisions.
3. **Creative Reflection:**
   This is a combination of the rational and the aesthetic. This is the key to music, visual arts, dance and higher order thinking skills.
4. **Intellectual Inquiry for Understanding:**
   We all learn but may not understand. To be a lifelong learner, one must value how and why, not only what.
5. **Engagement in Life:**
   Engagement with:
   - Projects and play
   - Teams and games
   - Community issues and giving
   - A sense of national spirit
   - International awareness
   - An ethical and moral life

Why digital fabrication?

The vision, mission and values of the school gave us the impetus to investigate digital fabrication and making. Our school is proud of the broad range of opportunities we provide to our students to not only learn across a range of disciplines but also to undertake experiential learning activities. Through participation in experiential activities, our students have the opportunity to develop their intellectual inquiry skills, build relationships with peers and teachers, and use their creative and critical thinking skills. We endeavour to provide opportunities which will enable our students to be courageous with their learning, expand their interests and develop their repertoire of skills. One example of experiential learning is our Howqua curriculum for Year 9 students. While at the Howqua campus, our Year 9 students participate in full academic and outdoor programmes. Through their participation in the Howqua programme, our students participate in hands-on activities and learn how to collaborate in teams and solve problems. They become more independent as thinkers and decision makers, particularly when they are given responsibility for planning all aspects of the hikes they participate in.

As a school we have come to value experiential or hands-on learning, and there is strong anecdotal evidence of students' improved self-confidence and ability to collaborate with others as a result. Our intention through this investigation of digital fabrication and making was to first determine ways in which we could further develop the experiential learning activities for our students, and second, consider how we might address the concern that girls are less likely to choose tertiary studies and careers related to science, technology, engineering and mathematics (STEM). We believe that using hands-on equipment and new technologies in a cross-disciplinary approach will assist our students in their learning and help them engage more effectively with STEM. Indeed, through teaching our students how to use and apply these technologies in innovative ways, we are supporting them in participating in a broad range of future careers and interests.

In 2013, while on study leave, I visited the Transformative Learning Technologies Lab at Stanford University's Graduate School of Education and met with Assistant Professor Paulo Blikstein. Professor Blikstein developed the concept of the Fablab@School, which supports project-based, student-centred learning; this is elaborated on in Chapter Six. The focus on invention, innovation and collaborative problem-solving was evident, and Professor Blikstein believes that students have the capacity to create inventions to solve real-world problems. I was able to visit the

Castilleja School for Girls in Palo Alto, where I observed a Fablab@School in action and students engaging in cross-disciplinary projects. Our school believes that students need to be exposed to hands-on activities in which they have the opportunity to solve real-life or authentic problems. Girls are good collaborators and they have the ability to solve problems, but they are not always exposed to hands-on activities. Our students already had the opportunity to undertake hands-on activities such as robotics, construction and tinkering-tables in classrooms, particularly in our Junior (Primary) School. The Fablab@School would enable us to further develop this work and progress current work into the Senior (Secondary) School, which begins in Year 7.

Lauriston Girls' School secured an arrangement with Stanford University's Graduate School of Education to establish a Fablab@School at our school; and with funding provided by the Lauriston Foundation, we opened the FabLab at the end of term 1 in 2014. Our FabLab coordinator is a teacher in our science faculty, and he has both teaching responsibilities within this faculty and a time allowance during the school day for collaborating with teachers and faculties on digital fabrication activities and projects.

A cross-disciplinary approach

We determined early in the establishment phase of the FabLab that this would be a cross-disciplinary space which would be available to students and teachers from Prep to Year 12. We firmly hold the view that our students need to be exposed to digital fabrication, design thinking, making and experiential activities from the early years of their primary education, in the same way they are exposed to science, mathematics and technology. We will be better able to engage students with these technologies and ways of thinking when they move into the secondary years of schooling and we provide broad access and multiple opportunities to undertake hands-on learning activities in the early years of a student's education journey.

As students move through Years 10 to 12, there are more constraints on teachers to maintain a content-rich curriculum and this can result in teacher concerns that cross-disciplinary activities, experiential and hands-on activities may take time away from ensuring that students have been taught all of the required content within a subject discipline. We have found that our Junior (Primary) School teachers and students have more flexibility within their curriculum to redefine units of work so that these include hands-on learning experiences in the digital fabrication laboratory.

Our primary school students engage with the equipment in the digital fabrication laboratory and the design thinking process being introduced to them with enthusiasm. We have observed similar levels of engagement and interest with our Year 7 and 8 students, who enjoy activities which offer broad, real-life problems or situations. These activities are less structured in terms of teacher-directed learning, with only limited guidance provided and a preference for students to resolve design issues and solve problems for themselves. The students are able to collaborate in groups, and our observations reveal their growing ability to manage when provided with a problem or situation with which they are not familiar and where failures are likely to arise. The digital fabrication laboratory provides an environment where our students will more than likely make mistakes, and these situations are both opportunities for learning and persevering to determine whether a workable solution can be found.

Our Visual Communication and Design students and our Art students in Years 11 and 12 use the digital fabrication laboratory equipment and this has expanded their creative capacity in design work and art pieces. Over the last two years, we have observed that students have been able to produce more refined design products and art works with multiple dimensions and new materials, which can be used in the laser cutter or 3D printer. For both primary and secondary students, we have observed the importance of the design element within all of the projects completed in the digital fabrication laboratory. Our students give equal value to the functionality and design features of the artefacts they produce.

Formal school curriculum

The following outline of the Year 10 STEM subject titled "Innovation Design Engineering" offers an insight into how our work in the digital fabrication laboratory has progressed. Our science teachers, including the teacher who became our FabLab coordinator, collaborated in the development of the elective, and with the opening of the FabLab, the elective has been able to progress. The elective subject began in Semester 2 in 2013 and was offered to students in Year 10 with the initial aim of increasing engagement in maths and science (in particular, physics and higher level mathematics) in Years 11 and 12.

Planning for the course began in November 2012 with the objective of developing an elective that would offer girls in Year 10 the opportunity to participate in a practical-based STEM course which would be linked to their classroom curricula in mathematics and science. The key ideas from an initial brainstorming meeting that formed the basis for the development of this course are listed below in table 1.

• Innovation Design & Technology • Goals: Enjoy, GET Curious • TimeLine: 15 weeks (35 lessons) • Stages: Robots, Analysis, Design (Engage, Explore, Extend) • Activity based – Present final project at assembly • Trips • Resources • Achievement / Assessment Portfolio, Projects-progressive, Presentation-final, Competency checks? • Connect with Math, Science, CAS.	• Sustainability: Address issues affecting people's lives • Engage: Robots-Programming-Hands on; simple; build; trial and error. • Explore: Use technology; characterise; robotics challenge; higher level robotics • Extend: Term 4 receive topic in term 3 to think through over the break. Design technology to address issue relevant to communities at the scales of the school, the state of Victoria, and internationally

Table 1 Initial brainstorming key words

From this meeting, the teachers developed a draft course outline and lesson plan. After many discussions, a final lesson plan was developed and rolled out in Semester 2, 2013.

First delivery of the Year 10 STEM elective (Semester 2, 2013)

The initial delivery of this course was a highly structured sequence with an emphasis on skill development through a series of predetermined activities for students. Only after these activities were completed was the major project introduced. The major project required the students to modify a prebuilt structure which would improve its ability to insulate against all forms of heat transfer using passive and active approaches. The passive approach involved using insulation the students developed from recycled materials while the active approach required the students to create a motor-driven window that could open and close using a switch they designed. The students could have as many switches as they needed to make the window open and close but the aim was to develop a reversible switch. A solar-powered circuit was also required to operate a fan to assist with cooling of the building.

Initially, all electric circuits were required to be run from a solar cell but due to the limited size and capacity of the solar cells available, this requirement was changed to having the solar cell running only a fan. The concept, however, was incorporated as an important aspect of sustainable house design.

The initial delivery of the course was conducted in the science classrooms. These rooms, purpose-built for conducting scientific experiments, were not the most suitable for the delivery of this type of practical-based course. The lab benches and student desks were not suited to the types of activities and building required for this course. To compensate, the students were supplied with a basic wooden structure (figure 12), and they were required to improve its capacity to control heat transfer. At this stage in the delivery of the course, the lack of suitable equipment, space and skill (in the teaching staff) to allow students to design and build their own house design necessitated this approach.

Figure 12 The basic wooden structure the first STEM class (Semester 2, 2013) was required to improve

The structure was made from 6mm plywood held together with metal brackets. A hinged window was present on one wall (not shown in this picture) and the roof was also hinged to allow access. The structure was attached to a larger wooden base (houses were designed by a science teacher in his home garage). An important phase of this project was to create an electrical circuit and switch that could open and close the window (Figure 13). The students were allowed to create any number of circuits and switches to ensure this could happen.

Figure 13 Reversing switch to drive 3V motor and gearbox (Semester 2, 2013), as an example of a switch that could both open and close the window by the operation of a single switching mechanism.

Students experimented with a range of recycled materials to create their own insulation. Material choices were based on the concepts that certain materials are naturally non-conductive, some materials are constructed with passive air gaps to reduce convection, and reflective materials are capable of controlling radiation (figure 14).

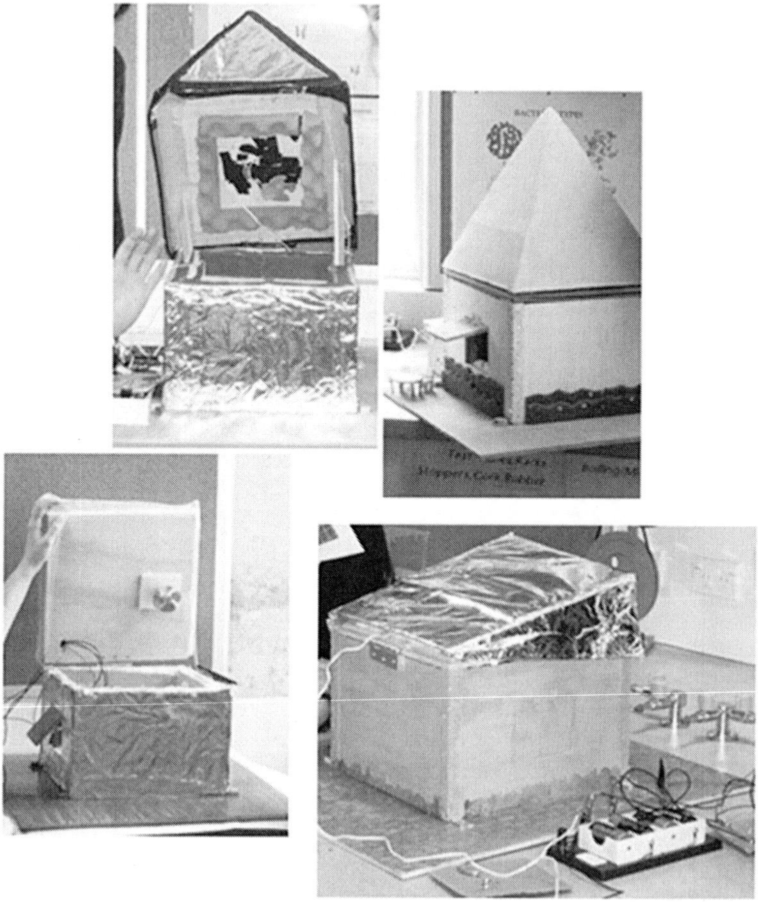

Figure 14 Finished houses from first cohort of students in Year 10 STEM elective (Semester 2, 2013)

Students modified a pre-set building structure to improve its capacity to control heat transfer into and out of the structure. An electric circuit was designed to control the opening and closing of the building window. A solar-powered circuit was designed to operate a fan to assist with the cooling of the building.

Outcomes

The final solutions developed by the students incorporated all the required elements of the brief and were functional in spite of limited materials and space in which to complete the activities. Student engagement in the activity was high, with a resultant variation in the solutions reached. Teamwork in completing this course was essential and this aspect of the learning became apparent very early on in the project. Discussions and debates about the way forward when solving a problem became the norm in this classroom. Helping others understand one's point of view through explanation and demonstration was also apparent.

Some issues of this first delivery of the Year 10 STEM elective

There were a number of issues which arose in the delivery of this course, many of which would be addressed in subsequent delivery of this course in the Lauriston FabLab. Some of the key issues are discussed below.

- The major issue of this project was that the students were unable to design and create their own house as the facilities were not available for the students to conduct any real type of construction work. The laboratory benches available were not equipped nor built in a way that allowed this type of work to be conducted. This meant that the students' imagining and innovation of the house they would like to build was limited. The students all felt a need to personalise their building and this was encouraged to build imagination and innovation.
- Materials for electronics were limited, so only simple switch-driven electric motors and gear systems were available to the students.
- Available power from our solar cells was limited, which required the use of an alternate power source (batteries) to run the main circuit (window motor).

Opening of the Lauriston fabrication laboratory (Term 1, 2014)

Prior to the delivery of the Year 10 STEM elective for the second time, the Lauriston fabrication laboratory was outfitted and opened. This fabrication laboratory was established in a classroom situated in the school's Science and Resource Centre. The classroom had access to air extraction, which was an important factor given the equipment to be used. In our planning of the space, we wanted to enable the delivery of construction-based learning activities across all year levels (P –12) and across all disciplines. An early decision was made to make this facility a cross-disciplinary space that would be made available to all year levels. This was important as no space of this kind existed anywhere else in the school. The outfitting of this space included the inclusion of digital design and manufacturing equipment (both 2D and 3D systems) and associated software, Arduino-based electronics and basic hand tools. During the setup of this facility, key staff was trained in the use of all equipment and software to allow classes to be conducted safely in this new learning environment.

Second delivery of the Year 10 STEM elective (Semester 2, 2014)

A repeat of the early introductory activities was undertaken to develop student confidence and direct their focus to the key elements they would need to include in their house design. New elements for their major project were introduced to address the limitations identified in the initial iteration of this course.

The following point was extracted from the modified major project brief.

- You will be required to design and develop:

1. A wooden house with wall and floor dimensions of: 30cm (L) x30cm (W) x20cm (H). You may use a flat roof or a pitched roof of no more than 20cm in height. You will have a land area of 50cm x 60cm on which to build your model.
2. An insulation material (passive) that can reduce all forms of heat transfer.
3. An Arduino computer control system that monitors temperature and opens and closes a window (active) to control the internal temperature of your house.
4. A solar power circuit that can run a fan (active).

Students were required to design their own house using Adobe Illustrator and then manufacture it using the laser cutter and hand tools. They were then required to insulate their house using recycled materials to achieve control of all three types of heat transfer (conduction, convection and radiation). A solar-powered circuit that could run a fan was again required. The new and exciting addition to this delivery of the course was the students' use of an Arduino computer system. The students would be required to design and build an electric circuit which would incorporate a temperature sensor, window motor and the Arduino computer. They would then be required to design and develop a computer program for the Arduino computer that would monitor the internal temperature of their house and open and close the window when a pre-set temperature was achieved.

Outcomes

The students created their own house designs but they were very limited in their approaches, with most structures being simple square buildings similar to the design used in the previous year (figure 15).

Figure 15 Students' initial design approach (Semester 2, 2014)

One group, however, incorporated different design elements, including the use of "living hinges" to create a curved roof rather than the standard flat or triangular-shaped roof elements. They also incorporated a circular window rather than a standard rectangular window (figure 16).

Figure 16 More innovative design approaches (Semester 2, 2014)

Student presentations of work became more digital-based and their design, construction and refining stages were documented in detail. Discussion of problems that arose and how they were solved (or not solved) were raised and dialogued upon during the student presentations.

Student ownership of their work was clearly apparent. Student confidence quickly developed and their problem-solving approach to their work became apparent. Students did not necessarily seek solutions to their problems but instead presented what they had discovered and how they might move forward. Unless an obvious need to redirect their approach was required, no input from the teacher – other than encouragement – was given.

The teachers' approach to student learning in this environment was to not offer solutions to problems but rather to ask questions to help them think about their approach/es. Encouragement and reassurance were needed in the early part of this approach to learning. As student confidence in their own abilities grew, the need for teacher input or the desire for teacher input decreased and a corresponding increase in student decision making and problem-solving skills increased. Students' ability to identify problems and carry out research to assist in solving problems also improved during this course.

Some issues of the second delivery of the Year 10 STEM elective

- The use of the 3V electric motor to open and close the window was problematic as it required many construction elements to convert the power of the motor into a force that would open and close the window.

Tight control over how long the motor was turning created many problems for the students.
    - This issue was addressed by the use of servo motors, which could be computer controlled to open through a pre-set range of motion ($0^{o} – 180^{o}$). Adjustment was only required in the computer program rather than in the construction of the motor, gears and timing of the motor.
- As student confidence in their abilities improved over the time of this course, the question arose as to whether the requirement of the students to complete the preliminary learning activities was necessary.
- Student house designs were clearly impacted by the previous designs they had seen. Only one group felt the confidence to try something different. This may have reflected simply school experiences with this type of activity. As new groups of students came through the system, they would have had more experiences using the FabLab and its equipment in other classes.

Subsequent deliveries of the Year 10 STEM elective (Semester 1 & 2, 2015; Semester 1, 2016)

Subsequent deliveries of this course over the last year and a half have seen an improvement in student approaches to completing this course. Students expect that they will be designing, developing and refining their own houses. They come prepared to deal with the teachers' expectation that they need to identify and solve their own problems. The students expect to work in teams and negotiate solutions to the satisfaction of all team members.

Introductory activities studying heat transfer, how insulation works, how solar cells work and basic kit construction are still occurring as a lead in to the students' major project. How to use Adobe Illustrator and the program in Arduino are now introduced earlier to allow the students more time to become confident with these programs. Interestingly, the most recent cohort had already had experiences designing with Illustrator when completing the Year 7 end-of-year STEM programme.

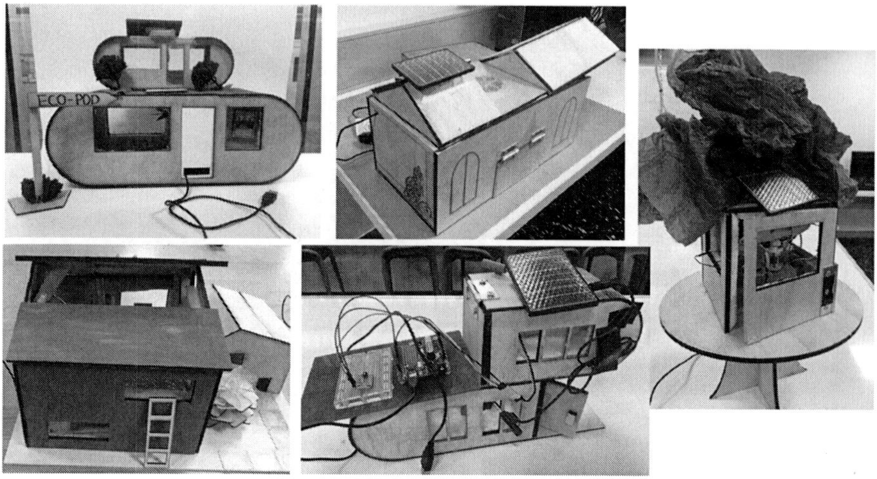

Figure 17 More innovative design approaches (2015 & 2016)

Students are now taking more risks with their house designs (figure 17). Originality of design and innovation in addressing the major project brief are occurring.

Figure 18 shows two examples from two separate groups of students having independently developed a computer-controlled solar cell that tracks the movement of the sun to maximise the energy received using supplemental Arduino boards.

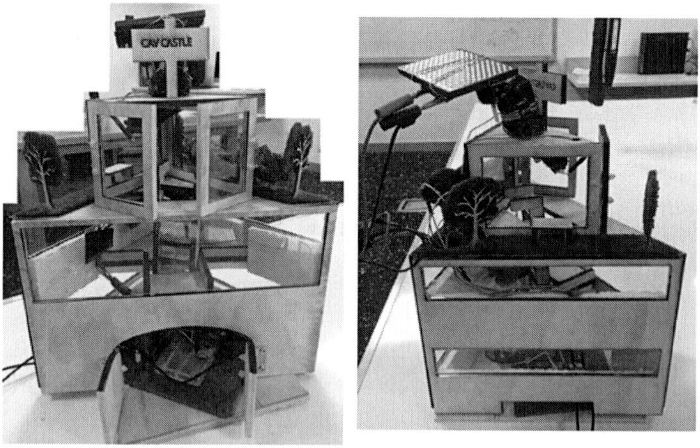

Figure 18 Innovation (2016)

Pedagogical benefits and future challenges

We believe that the Year 10 STEM elective has made significant progress, and as more students become familiar with the digital fabrication laboratory and have consistent access to it, their skills and approaches will continue to enhance their final products. When we consider the other projects which have been completed in the digital fabrication laboratory since 2014, we can observe this refinement of original concepts. It is reasonable that teachers will always refine projects after the initial implementation with students. Within the digital fabrication laboratory, however, there is also a growing confidence on the part of teachers about how they can use the equipment and an awareness of the skills and abilities our students already have. For example, in a recent Year 7 and 8 lantern-making project, the students were required to solder points on an electrical circuit. We had not previously taught the students how to solder but they managed to successfully undertake this task.

One of the valuable lessons we have learnt on our journey to date is the importance of sharing knowledge and skills. In 2016, we invited two colleagues from the USA to work with our students for one week in our digital fabrication laboratory. Our FabLab coordinator described the two weeks with our colleagues as valuable professional learning. Working together, they were able to share information about different projects undertaken, discuss equipment and materials which had been used, and share their stories of classroom experiences. The sharing of classroom experiences is important because we can learn more about what is possible with students and the types of environments conducive to achieving successful student outcomes.

There are challenges that we face as we continue to embed digital fabrication, making and design thinking in our school curriculum. We have observed that our primary years' teachers have more opportunities to redefine their curriculum, which has resulted in the continued development of projects that utilise the digital fabrication laboratory. A number of interdisciplinary projects have been developed and are being further refined each year, and new interdisciplinary projects are being planned. For example, the teacher developing the Year 1 interdisciplinary project where students are digitally designing and building fairy houses has progressed her work with the same students, who in their Prep year digitally designed pyramids. Our students are developing skills and dispositions regarding digital fabrication, design thinking and making from an early age, and it is reasonable that they will continue to be engaged in interdisciplinary projects and further enhance their skills and understanding as their education progresses at the school. As these students move into the middle years of secondary school, we envisage that their acquired skills and understanding will provide impetus for teachers and faculties (departments) to redefine aspects of the curriculum and ensure the continued design and delivery of interdisciplinary, project-based learning opportunities.

Professional learning linked directly to project-based learning, interdisciplinary approaches, digital pedagogies and use of equipment in the digital fabrication laboratory will continue at our school. Teachers who are advocates of digital fabrication, making and design thinking will have more success in bringing their colleagues along the journey, particularly when these individuals are able to share their work and highlight the outcomes achieved for their students. The sharing of projects that successfully demonstrate interdisciplinary approaches will be important in order to maintain the dialogue with teachers about digital fabrication, making and design thinking.

In choosing to take such an interdisciplinary approach, we have taken a more challenging path in that faculties (departments) or subject disciplines must choose to redefine their current subject discipline curriculum to incorporate digital fabrication and design thinking or develop an interdisciplinary unit of work across faculties. The alternative would be to adjust the current timetable and include a specific number of lessons per cycle, which would enable the development of a curriculum based around digital fabrication, design thinking and making. There are schools in Australia and the USA where a STEAM (science, technology, engineering, arts, mathematics) subject discipline has been introduced in the primary years of schooling and older students have access to compulsory or elective courses. While we have chosen to persist with our current approach, we will be undertaking an audit of the primary years' curriculum to determine how and where digital technology, making and design thinking may be included in current units of work and topics of study. In the secondary years, it is likely that digital fabrication and design thinking will form part of the work to be undertaken to enhance the technology curriculum offered to students. As a result of this work, students from Years 7 to 9 will have a dedicated number of hours each Semester in which an interdisciplinary project will be completed, with a focus on the use of design thinking, digital technologies and digital fabrication.

Another challenge for our school is how we will introduce digital fabrication, making and design thinking at our rural Howqua campus. The Howqua campus for Year 9 students is relatively technology-free, with the students having limited access to digital devices during the school day. They do not bring their own digital devices to the campus. Consistent with the central philosophy of Howqua, there are other priorities, including building communication and team skills, developing empathy and understanding for others, learning how to live and work with peers and finding one's own character strengths and those of others through the outdoor and fitness programmes. We are currently developing a plan which will enable broader use of technologies in the classroom without diminishing the technology-free elements within this residential community. Digital fabrication, making and woodwork would enable opportunities for project-based learning and enhance the development of resilience and independence, which are at the foundation of the Year 9 Howqua programme.

Next steps

Our digital fabrication laboratory has been in operation since 2014, and while there has been progress, we believe that it will take up to five years to establish a more consistent utilisation of the FabLab within the primary and secondary school. The laboratory should become part of the digital pedagogical toolkit for teachers. This will require teachers to learn new skills and redefine current projects within their subject disciplines. We would aim for students to value the digital fabrication laboratory as a place where they can undertake hands-on projects and activities with limited guidance from their teachers and opportunities to determine the knowledge and skills they will need for successful completion of their project.

Case studies and research will form part of the next phase of our work regarding digital fabrication, making and design thinking. While access to digital fabrication, making and design thinking may not result in an increase in the number of our students studying science and mathematics in their senior years of schooling, or studying STEM-related courses at a tertiary institute, we believe there are worthwhile avenues of research to pursue over the longer time frame. We would like to undertake a longitudinal study to determine whether there is an increased uptake in science and mathematics at the senior years of schooling as a result of the access to digital fabrication from the early years of primary education. Research of cohorts from primary to the secondary years would enable us to make observations about the engagement and interest levels of students in their STEM-related subjects. An interesting aspect to this research will be the opportunities to compare the attitudes and engagement levels towards STEM-related subjects in the new students who join the school at

Year 7 and may not previously have had the opportunity to engage in digital fabrication in their early years of schooling.

Other studies on interdisciplinary projects which utilise digital fabrication and how these projects are assessed would augment current thinking on the nature of assessment in this area. Another area for research would be to consider a longitudinal study on the impact student participation in interdisciplinary, project-based learning has on approaches to learning, such as collaboration, self-regulation, critical and creative thinking, and reflections on learning.

As educators in a school, we understand that we are preparing our students for a rapidly changing world. The process of learning is no longer focused on the acquisition of knowledge but rather the acquisition of a set of skills that will enable students to think creatively and critically, to reflect on their learning and to collaborate and communicate effectively with others. The digital fabrication laboratory provides an environment for our students in which these skills can be developed along with the dispositions of perseverance, resilience in the face of obstacles and mistakes, curiosity and self-motivation. We have an opportunity as a school to continue our work in digital fabrication, making and design thinking and create a learning environment for our students that fosters skills and dispositions for the 21st century. The next chapter takes up the theme of these skills, competencies and dispositions and applies them to transboundary contexts of learning.

Appendix 1: Other Projects Conducted in FabLab

2014 – Construction and Development Phase

- Prep students used iPads to create a personal design for their "100 days at school" medal. Their designs were cut out on the laser cutter.
- Year 7 – end-of-year STEM project – The Fabulous Christmas Toy
- Year 10 STEM elective – Sustainable house design incorporating computerisation (Arduino boards) to monitor house temperature and operate a motor to open and close a window. Students used Illustrator and a laser cutter to create their own design. Students used the FabLab to create their houses; the science classroom was not used for construction.

2015 – First Year of Full Operation

- Prep students used iPads to designed pyramids as a part of their cross-disciplinary study looking at history, maths (3D shapes) and design. Their designs were cut out on the laser cutter.
- Prep students used iPads to create a personal design for their "100 days at school" medal.
- Year 1 students fabricated Chinese calligraphy – using iPads and laser cutter.
- Year 4 students fabricated Chinese calligraphy - using Illustrator and laser cutter.
- Year 6 students participated in an Immigration study and used Illustrator and the laser cutter, as well as receiving an introduction to 3D designing and printing.
- Years 5 and 6 Maths Extension – Introduction to Computer programing using Arduino boards.
- Year 7 – end-of-year STEM project – The Fabulous Christmas Toy.
- Year 8 Geography – Contour mapping study using 3D designing and printing.
- Year 10 STEM elective – Sustainable house design incorporating computerisation (Arduino boards) to monitor house temperature and operate a servo-motor to open and close a window. Students used Illustrator and the laser cutter to create their own design. Students used FabLab to create their houses; the science classroom was not used for construction.
- Year 11 Psychology – Model of the eye.

- Individual Year 12 students worked on a range of projects for their Visual Communication and Design and Art courses of study.
- Set production (houses and makeup stencils) for Senior School production of Our Town.

2016 – Second Year of Full Operation

- Prep students used iPads to design a shoe key-ring as an extension of their cross-disciplinary study involving design. Their designs were cut out on the laser cutter.
- Prep students used iPads to create a personal design for their "100 days at school" medal.
- Year 1 STEM Activity: "The fairies at the bottom of the garden". Students are using iPads to design a house following the requirements requested in a letter from the fairies. This is a cross-disciplinary project (language arts, mathematics, design, construction, technology) using iPads and the laser cutter. Prototyping, redesigning and final production are all required. An extension to this project is the use of Squishy circuits to light the houses.
- Year 6 students have completed an Introduction to Illustrator and the laser cutter project, and will use Illustrator and the laser cutter in their Immigration study
- Year 10 STEM elective – Sustainable house design incorporating computerisation (Arduino boards) to monitor house temperature and operate a servo-motor to open and close a window. Students use Illustrator and the laser cutter to create their own design. Students use FabLab to create their houses; the science classroom was not used for construction.
- Set production (phones) for Senior School Musical production of "Bye Bye Birdie".
- Individual Year 12 students work on a range of projects for Visual Communication and Design and Art courses.
- Year 7 students will participate in the end-of-year STEM project – The Fabulous Christmas Toy.
- Year 8 students will undertake a contour mapping study in Geography using 3D designing and printing.
- Year 10 French students will apply their language skills whilst utilising the facilities of the FabLab.

CHAPTER THREE

BRIDGING TRANSBOUNDARY SPACES THROUGH MAKING

MICHAEL VALLANCE

Introduction

As the preceding chapter has shown, makerspaces, fabrication labs and 3D printing facilities are becoming widespread in spaces of learning, including in higher education institutes. In addition, many universities worldwide are attempting to "internationalise" their student community. This situation provides a favourable opportunity to consider innovative applications to support "new learning" (Kalantzis and Cope, 2012) embracing multi-disciplinary education and multi-cultural creativity by multiple users across diverse environments. To do so requires educators to bridge transboundary spaces, which can be done through technology. One such technology is virtual reality.

The chapter begins with a rationale for Social Constructivism as a relevant theory of knowledge for "new learning" in a digitally connected society. This is then developed for more active, participatory learning situations proposed by Seymour Papert and Idit Harel (1993); termed Constructionism. Virtual reality is then summarised as a platform upon which to enact Constructionism in an era of transformative education unrestricted by international borders. The context for a particular application of Constructionism in this instance is called robot-mediated interactions. The justification for using robots and virtual spaces is subsequently explained. Five implementations of virtual reality architectures in real-world educational use are then summarised. A commentary by a student using virtual reality to design, make and 3D print real-world objects is additionally illustrated. The chapter concludes with a discussion of applying Constructionism in learner-centred 3D virtual reality designs, bridging transboundary spaces.

Social Constructivism, Constructionism and virtual spaces

Cognitive science is acknowledged as the interdisciplinary study of mind and intelligence. It is important as it attempts to explain how the mind works. The central hypothesis of cognitive science is, "Thinking can best be understood in terms of representational structures in the mind and computational procedures that operate on those structures" (Thagard 2005, 10); the computer analogy being data structures plus algorithms result in operating programs. How the mind works is often explained by cognitive scientists in terms of logic, rules, concepts, analogies, images and neural connections (Thagard 2005). In the 1960s and 70s, learners were thought of as "intelligent systems" and the term "metacognition"(awareness of thinking processes and "executive control" of such processes) fell in line with the "brain as a computer" metaphor. However, recent studies in neuroscience reveal that learning is far more complex. Wider issues of social relationships, contexts, feelings and personal goals have been recognised as impacting learning (Vygotsky 1986; Papert 1993; Dede 1996). A credible theory of learning to support a more cognitive science-friendly course of study, informed by quantitative and qualitative data worldwide (Wiliam 2011), is called Social Constructivism (Piaget 1972).

Social Constructivism does not prescribe wholly planned strategies of instruction but promotes learning environments that provide opportunities to engage learners in meaning making. It supports active learning processes of accommodation (accepting new experiences) and assimilation (making sense of new experiences based upon what is known). Accordingly, technology is used in higher education to actuate multimodal, multiple media representations of information that require students to develop multi-literacies for meaningful knowledge development (Kress 2013). A number of courses in progressive universities around the world are implemented based upon the theories of multimodality, with implementation informed by Social Constructivism. There is less of an emphasis on "learning about" content knowledge and more on experiences of "learning in and for" an unpredictable future (Kalantzis and Cope 2012); for instance, community, curricula and pedagogy at the MIT Media Lab exemplify Social Constructivism's prolific creativity.

In addition to the theory of Social Constructivism, research has revealed that effective learning occurs when students are "active producers" of learning. This is termed Constructionism (Papert and Harel 1993). Knowledge is not merely a commodity to be transmitted, encoded and retained but personal experience to be actively constructed. In an indirect endorsement of Constructionism, Kolb (1984, 41) asserts that learning is considered to be a "process whereby knowledge is created through the transformation of experience". Vallance and Towndrow (n.d.) reasoned that a practical implementation for such active, experiential and multi-disciplinary learning is for students to consider, analyse, solve and extract personal meaning from engaging problems. Multi-disciplinary problem solving presents opportunities for reciprocation between declarative and procedural knowledge in which personal input and collaborative efforts support cognitive connections that can lead to an understanding of concepts and theories in multiple contexts (i.e., meta-cognitive knowledge). Additionally, collaborative problem-solving promotes communication involving creative and interpretive meaning-making, analysis and reflective judgement (Tarricone 2011). A pedagogical and learning approach that encourages exploration, procedural knowledge, iterative, recursive and logical thinking, structured task breakdown, and dealing with abstraction is therefore required.

Virtual reality (and 3D virtual spaces) offers a possible context for developing this "new learning". Dalgarno et al. (2002, 152) state: "By exploring and manipulating a 3D virtual environment the learner will develop a spatial model of the concepts represented and that, for certain types of concepts, this spatial model is central to thorough conceptual understanding". Sara deFreitas and Tim Neumann (2009) suggest that the appeal, immersivity and immediacy of virtual worlds can support "experiential learning" but education requires a re-consideration of how, what, when and where we learn. They use John Dewey's concept of inquiry to propose that learners' virtual experiences, their use of multiple media, the transactions and activities between peers, and the facilitation of learner control between them will lead to "transactional learning" that "aims to support deeper reflection upon the practices of learning and teaching", which arguably leads to "wider opportunities for experiential learning" (ibid).

Such opportunities can take the form of highly defined tasks. Programming of robots, for instance, provides the necessary comparability and empirical data to determine the success of task completion (Barker and Ansorge 2007; Vallance and Martin 2012). For example, the programming of a robot to navigate mazes of measurable complexity can be adopted (Papert 1993; Vallance et al. 2013). Research can be designed to observe students communicating in a 3D virtual space while programming a robot to follow distinct challenges that, in turn, result in tangible and quantifiably measured outcomes. To meet these criteria, LEGO Mindstorms EV3 robot programming components can be used to quantify task complexity and thus iteratively increase the challenges given to high school and undergraduate university students. Additionally, a 3D virtual simulation provides interesting, engaging and realistic yet safe contexts where robots are ordinarily utilised; e.g., disaster recovery and search and rescue situations. A virtual simulation allows remotely located students to enter as avatars to communicate and collaborate with other students. Data within the environment can also be captured for analysis. Specifically, researchers and educators need to find ways to evaluate experiences of activities and collaboration in 3D virtual spaces, and provide awareness of the benefits and challenges of working in 3D virtual-to-real augmented environments.

It was therefore decided to utilise 3D virtual reality as an experiential stage to engage learners in the programming of robots to undertake specific tasks supported by a Constructionist theory of learning. In the next section, five virtual world architectures and one virtual craft design will be discussed.

Making and applying virtual scenarios to bridge transboundary spaces

The student makers in this project adopted the Successive Approximation Model (SAM) to design, construct and implement their 3D virtual creations. SAM is a development model that uses a continuous iterative process to design, make and play. This was deemed more effective than using the traditional Instructional Design standard ADDIE model (Analysis, Design, Development, Implementation and Evaluation). The ADDIE model was considered limiting as each stage would have had to be corrected before moving onto the next stage. The SAM model allows for more diverse, creative, innovative and unusual possibilities during the creative process as opposed to an evaluation at the end of a process.

Each virtual architecture scenario has been supported by metaverse designers and educators involved in the robot-mediated interactions research project. A descriptive analysis of the constructed scenarios is provided below. In each implementation, a purposive group of students in Japan, Wales (UK) and the USA designed, constructed, tested and participated in unique virtual world tasks. References to published articles detailing the quantitative and qualitative data that have informed the research outcomes are provided.

Robot-mediated interaction and Second Life

The initial research, from 2010 to 2012, utilised the Second Life virtual world and LEGO NXT Mindstorms robots. The design of the virtual learning space by participating students enabled individual avatars to place and move NXT Mindstorms software blocks on a virtual floor. These blocks were semiotic representations of the software components required to build the program necessary to manoeuvre the LEGO robot in pre-determined task circuits. On the sides of the virtual structures were images of the software configuration panels. These were displayed so that students could point and focus on commands and variables that needed to be input in order to program specifically detailed operations of the robots.

Once the virtual learning space had been built by the students, 16 tasks were implemented: the initial seven were utilised for practice and data was collected from the remaining nine. Each iteratively more difficult task aimed to challenge students to communicate a construction process leading to a successful outcome; that is, program a LEGO robot to follow a specified circuit of movements and turns. Communication between participants (in this case, N=8) was supported by the virtual world chat facility and the behaviour of participants' avatars in the environment.

For each task, teams in the UK and Japan had to physically reconstruct the maze on the floor of their laboratory using adhesive tape. Next, one team's task was to act as "learners" and create a robot program (using the Mindstorms software) to follow the maze that the other "teaching" team had designed. The learning team used the information provided in the Second Life space in an attempt to solve the robot programming problem. Over 60 hours of video capture of participants communicating in the real world were recorded, transcribed and analysed. Details of the research may be found in Vallance and Martin (2012).

In summary, given the steadily rising level of task difficulty and the students' increasing mastery of the more challenging tasks, as evidenced by their ability to complete them with fewer errors and in less time, Bloom's taxonomy of educational objectives (Anderson et al. 2001) suggests that some developmental pattern should be expected to emerge as the procedural knowledge required to complete the tasks came to be more effectively applied as student accomplishment increased. However, the relative frequency with which particular kinds of cognition appeared in the data (e.g., "applying procedural knowledge") was not patterned as tasks progressed and difficulty increased. Moreover, the relative frequency with which the different elements of cognition appeared in the data (e.g., "applying conceptual knowledge") did not present itself as the linear or rising percentage expected in a developmental sequence. Our data showed that learning is not as structured or uniform as Bloom's taxonomy suggests. This motivated us to seek further insights by considering alternative 3D spaces.

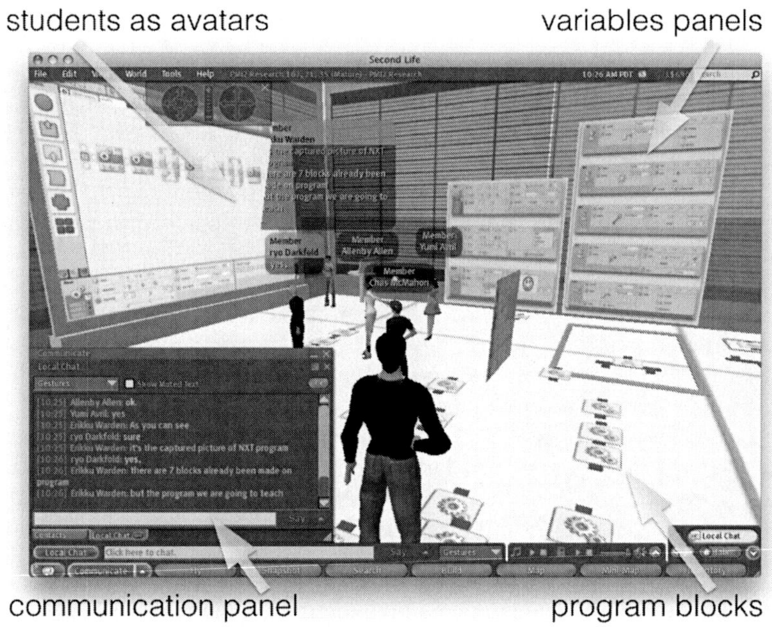

Figure 19 Constructing NXT robot program blocks in Second Life

Robot-mediated interaction and OpenSim

At this juncture, OpenSim was chosen over Second Life due to financial and privacy protection considerations. Our learner-centred design approach enabled a number of innovative tools to be created and customised by the students in OpenSim; for instance, the ability to move a graphical representation of the LEGO robot object and leave a trace of the circuit in-world. Also, media objects in-world displayed live streamed video from the lab in Japan and also from an iPhone attached to the front of the LEGO robot. Virtual noticeboards were also updated with text and images to aid communication. Details of the research may be found in Vallance et al. (2013).

Tragically, on March 11, 2011, a catastrophic tsunami badly damaged the reactor cooling systems at the Fukushima Daiichi nuclear plant in Japan. Reactor units exploded and radioactivity was released to the atmosphere. The consequences of the Fukushima accident remain even today: many evacuees cannot return home, depression is becoming prevalent among the strained residents, workers are struggling to maintain the safety of the plant, millions of litres of contaminated water are being stored on-site, and deformities have been discovered in local wildlife. One of the most surprising technology-related episodes during the early post-disaster efforts was the lack of robots in Japan to assist with the recovery operations. These events motivated undergraduate students at Future University, Hakodate, Japan to take ownership of the design, iterative development and construction of a 3D virtual space where participants can be involved in simulated disaster recovery using robots. The result, in the context of this research, is that remotely located students in Japan and Wales, UK were able to collaborate in solving specific tasks of measurable complexity within a disaster-themed environment built in OpenSim.

Learning data was collected from 2013 to 2014, when the participants were undergraduate students studying Media Architecture in a Systems Information Science-focused Japanese university (N=6) and A-level students in the UK studying science-based subjects (N=10). Of the 16 participants, 2 were female, 14 were male; all were aged between 17 and 19 and no one had any prior experience working with the project's technologies. Some tasks involved Japanese students collaborating with other remotely located Japanese students, and others with Japanese students collaborating with the UK students. Tasks included manoeuvring the Mindstorms robots around obstacles using "distance" and "turn" commands, using touch sensors to find ways around obstacles, constructing a bridge and using touch sensors to move over obstacles, using light sensors to avoid obstacles and using sensors to locate items. Communication between students required the use of virtual-world tools such as text panes, voice, live video streaming of respective real-world labs, and 3D presentation boards.

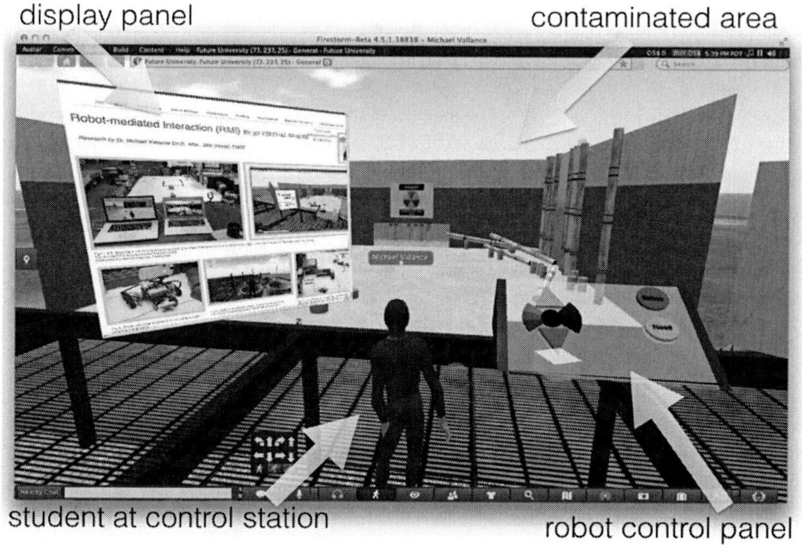

Figure 20 An example of a control station in OpenSim

As the collaborative tasks became more complex, the students indicated that even though the tasks were considered demanding, they deemed their skills to be competent, thereby indicating some degree of learner development. However, in later tasks the students revealed that as the level of challenge increased (from manageable to difficult), their skill level in attempting to seek successful outcomes decreased (from competent to reasonable). Looking at the task communication transcripts and screen captures, it appears that the students had to utilise different procedural knowledge involving, for instance, programming a touch sensor to coordinate with a motor action. These latter tasks required students to analyse and create unique solutions based upon their prior task experiences, and were thus deemed most challenging. The increased task complexity necessitated a higher level of programing skill incorporating sensor variables and loops. Even though students' post-task reflection data revealed that they found sensor-related tasks difficult, being immersed in a task led to more active learning and, in turn, led to greater student success. Details of the research may be found in Vallance et al. (2015).

To further enhance the interactivity within the OpenSim space, a National Instruments' LabView VI program was developed to enable communication directly between an in-world object and the physical

LEGO robot. This resulted in the UK students controlling avatars in the OpenSim virtual environment to subsequently remotely manoeuvre a real-world LEGO robot physically located in Japan as an additional "search and rescue" simulated task (*cf.* Arnold 2012). To augment this tele-robotic capability, students connected a LEAP Motion Controller (www.leapmotion.com) for hands-free remote manoeuvring of the robot. Without physically touching the computer screen or a controller, students could hover their hand or fingers over the OpenSim avatar to control and then manoeuvre the wirelessly connected robot, as shown in figure 21. Students would later return to the potential of the LEAP Motion Controller for virtual crafting and 3D printing.

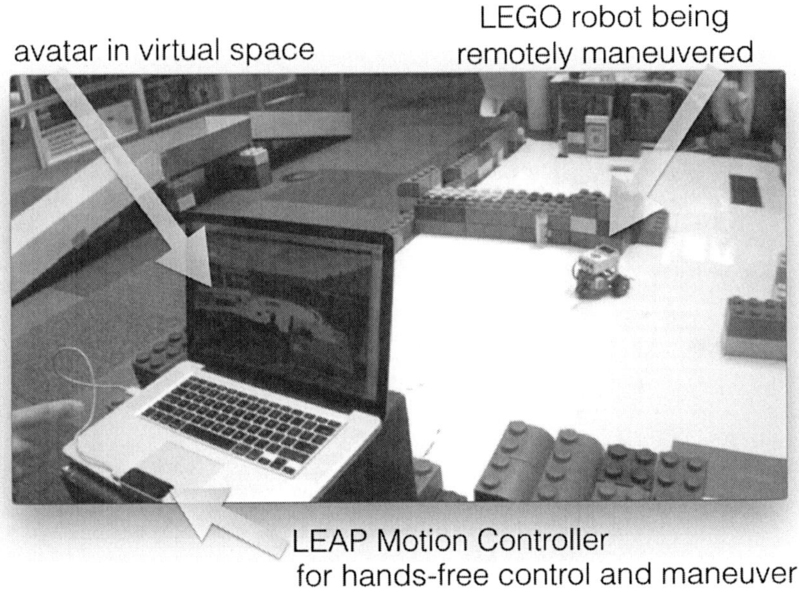

Figure 21 LEAP Motion controller being used for the remote manoeuvring of an EV3 robot via the OpenSim Training Area

Robot-mediated interaction and OpenQwaq

During 2014, a global virtual team collaboration project between first-year university students in the United States (N=20) and Japan (N=7) utilising the OpenQwaq 3D virtual environment was implemented (see fig.

22). Students in both locations met synchronously within the 3D virtual space over the course of four weeks, and were challenged with collaborating to discover solutions to robot tasks. One location each week designed a robot task that was shared with the other classroom at the start of the online meeting. The class that was challenged could ask the students at the other location questions to help them understand the construction and subsequently program the robot sensors to complete the task. The OpenQwaq forum supported several beneficial tools for virtual team collaboration, including text chat and synchronous audio and video feeds from both locations. The physical layout of the 3D space resembled a real-world conference room, with panels placed on the walls to display live video camera feeds, such as a full-room view and a close-up view of the robots performing the tasks, from each site. A discussion panel was used to provide a text chat for students to ask and answer questions.

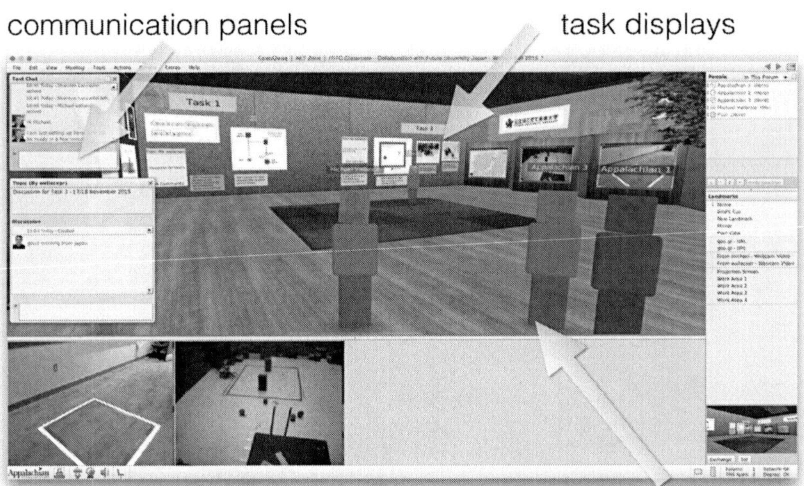

Figure 22 Interactions in OpenQwaq

Robot-mediated interaction and Unity 3D

In 2015, a Unity designer created a much more realistic virtual nuclear plant for the researchers and students to adapt. The 3D space replicates the real-world Fukushima nuclear reactors with cooling towers prior to the disaster of March 2011. The user-accessible simulation, with learners and members of the public controlling the virtual robot, aims to create an awareness and understanding of disaster recovery, and not simply rely upon retrospective information from unprepared experts. Consequently, as well as capturing data for analysis of cognitive processes, the affective aim was to familiarise students and the public with the complexities of nuclear power, given that there is much confusion about the situation at present in Japan. The pedagogic rationale was to combine a 3D simulation space for real-world collaboration; in this case, the programming of robots contextualised by simulating a robot navigating within a restricted area. As the project matures, students and adults gain hands-on experience moving around the simulated virtual Fukushima space and observe a physical robot simultaneously moving at a remote location (e.g., in a scaled mock-up of a hazardous building such as the reactor).

To additionally engage the learners in the active design and construction of their learning environment, in both the 3D space and the real-world lab, a virtual abandoned factory space was designed for initial training and familiarity with 3D virtual manoeuvres, interactions and “emotion-mind” conflict that often results in motion sickness. Students manoeuvre the virtual robot using the built-in controller to pick up radioactive bins. A radiation meter in the bottom right corner indicates radioactivity levels that provide a clue as to the nearness of the radioactive bins. A rear-view mirror for the robot controller is viewed in the top right corner. A birds-eye view is offered via a virtual drone that can be manoeuvred over the abandoned factory, seeking out the location of the radioactive bins (see fig. 23). If the robot crashes, the radioactive bins explode. Upon successful completion of the Abandoned Factory scenario, students are teleported to the Fukushima nuclear power plant scenario (see figs. 24, 25). Details of the research may be found in Vallance and Ibayashi (2015).

Figure 23 Interface and controls

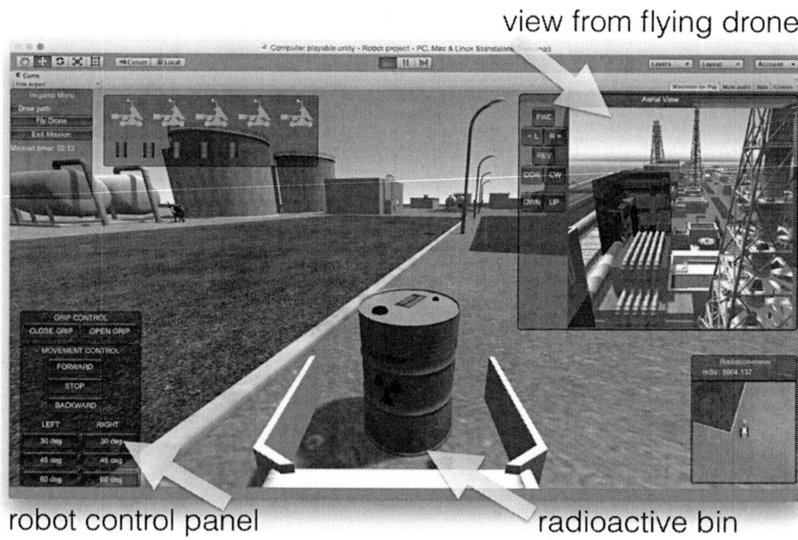

Figure 24 Robot retrieving a radioactive bin in virtual Fukushima

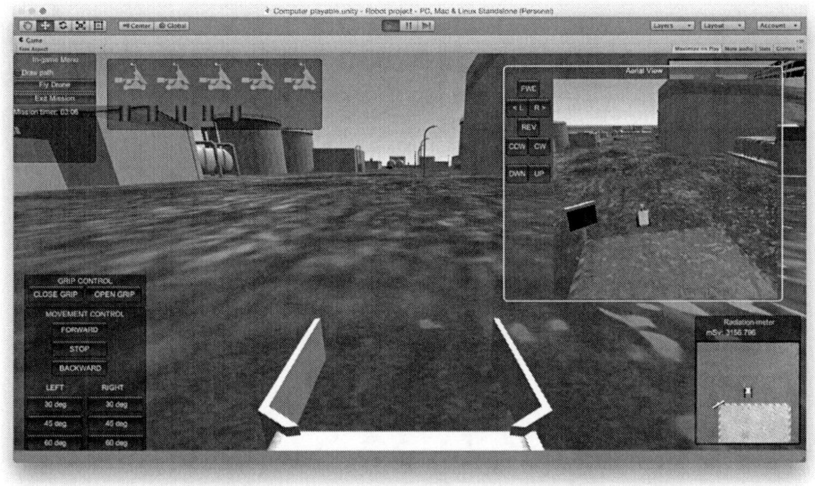

Figure 25 Tsunami flooding in virtual Fukushima

Robot-mediated interaction with Oculus Rift

The Unity project was also developed to be viewable via the Oculus Rift 3D head-mounted display (see fig. 26). Students manoeuvre the virtual robot using the built-in controller to locate and pick up the radioactive bins. It is anticipated that future commercial developments in virtual reality technologies will enable users to log in to online 3D virtual spaces to engage and collaborate with other remotely located participants; bridging transboundary spaces while fully immersed in impossible places and magical worlds. Technologies include not only the head-mounted displays exemplified in this research by the Oculus Rift but also immersive virtual reality environments known as CAVE (Cave Automatic Virtual Environment). The maturation of immersive technologies has profound implications for the design and implementation of higher education and its subsequent pedagogies, curricula and assessments. Engaging students to conduct research in future virtual reality scenarios will better inform and prepare for such profound changes in education, learning, curricula and pedagogy.

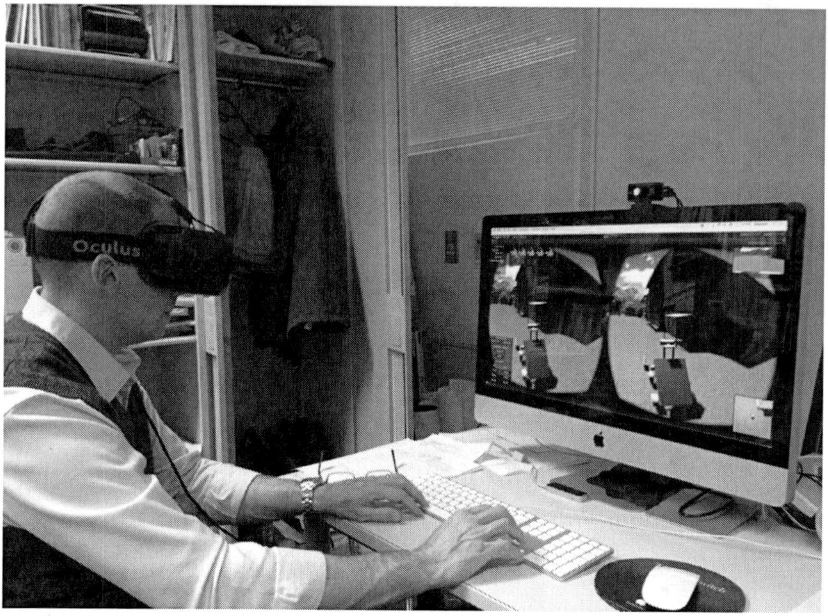

Figure 26 Manoeuvring a robot in Oculus Rift

Virtual Craft

To enhance the use of virtual spaces and the Maker concept, one of the students opted to develop a 3D space to design and then print, on a 3D printer, virtually created objects. This portion of the project is reported in the words of the student, Kenta Ibayashi.

> In this study I proposed Virtual Craft, which allows users to create 3D objects. This project was based on playing with LEGO blocks because it is a popular creative artifact. I developed two virtual prototypes. The first used a Microsoft Kinect as the Natural User Interface (NUI) device. The second used a Leap Motion Controller added to the Oculus Rift in order to produce virtual reality.
>
> In the prototype, there are walls, a floor, a table, LEGO blocks, and boxes that duplicate blocks. It is just like a real room in a real world, which is created to intense immersion (see fig. 27). Also, users can control a spherical object that follows a user's hand. By controlling the object as a pointer, users can do crafting.

To use Virtual Craft, users only use their right hand, taking blocks from boxes and putting them on the table to complete the 3D object. Two kinds of blocks are prepared: a green square and a red cuboid. When the sphere touches a block, the block becomes disengaged from the sphere and becomes part of the 3D object. Users can make 3D objects by repeating this process. This is based on a process of LEGO crafting in the real world, so even those unfamiliar with information technology device are able to do such creation.

Also, the designed Virtual Craft VR space uses feedback from sounds that inform users what is happening in Virtual Craft. When blocks touch the table or other blocks, they make a sound, signalling the completion of putting the blocks in order. This was found to reduce human error as there is no tactile perception in VR.. 3D objects on a 2D screen are usually made using a keyboard and mouse, and users have to rotate objects in order to see the depth of 3D objects. In 2D spaces such as the computer display, users are forced to do such tiring operations. This study allows users to recognize the depth of 3D objects in real time with VR, and it leaves out operations concerning depth recognition. Once a 3D object has been completed, it can be exported directly to a real-world 3D printer. An example of a 3D-printed object designed and built in the VR space is shown in figures 28 and 29.

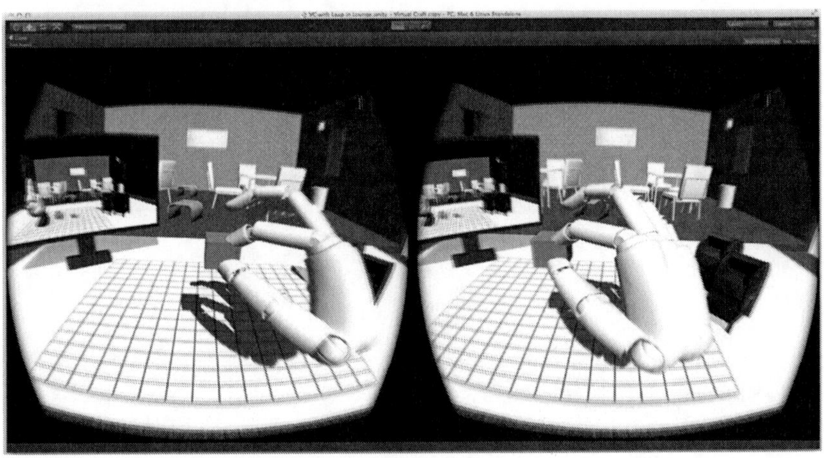

Figure 27 Virtual craft using LEAP and Oculus Rift

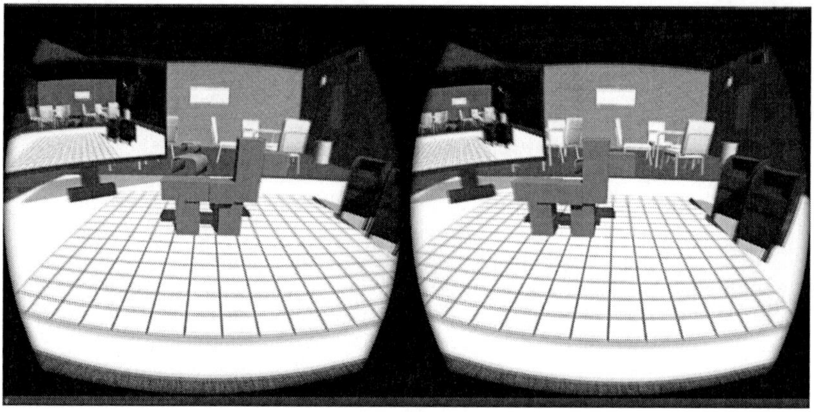

Figure 28 A 3D object created in virtual space

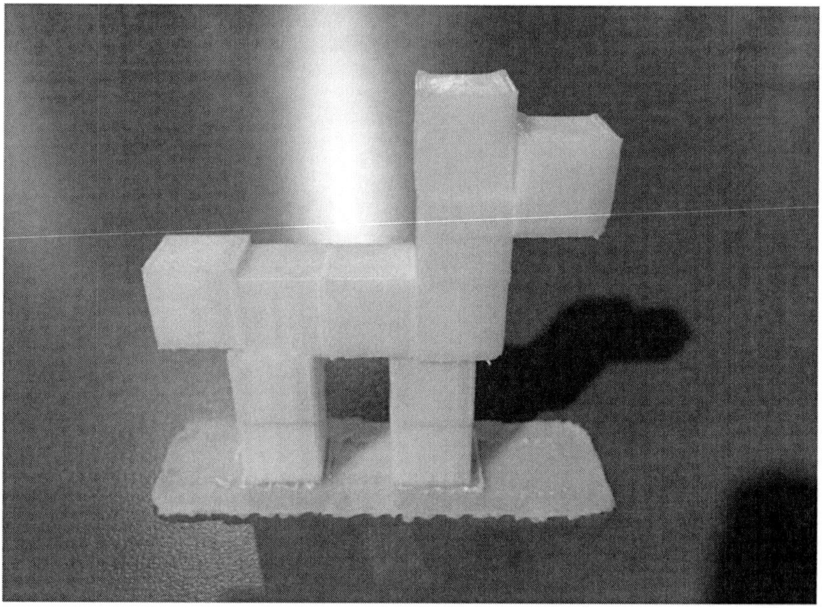

Figure 29 A 3D object printed using a 3D printer

Discussion

The chapter has summarised and exemplified a Constructionist-informed blending of virtual spaces and real-world education applications. It has been found that educators considering the use of virtual reality must give deliberate consideration to the aim and goals of the designed space, its intended learning outcomes, the cognitive load associated with the activities, the instructional strategies, the motivation of the users, the affordances offered by the space and activities and, if relevant, the user assessment criteria. In addition, virtual spaces need to be engaging, intuitive and satisfying. As Koenig et al. (2013, 49) state: "The simple presence of educational content in a simulation does not guarantee its efficacy". Moreover, this long-term project has highlighted the importance of reflection, feedback, de-briefing and after-action reviews.

Everyday interactions involve the use of semiotics as signs or symbols that evoke meaning through culture and context (Catlin et al., 2010). The benefit of using the LEGO Mindstorms robot is its semiotic programming interface. Users communicate their ideas to a robot via its Mindstorms programming interface according to specific programming syntax. The robots' actions in turn provide feedback to the user through its movements. This semiotic system has been replicated in the virtual spaces (as shown in the scenarios in Sect. 3) to facilitate such robot-mediated interactions.

Increased active learner participation has been informed by a Constructionist theory of learning. Immersion (often termed flow (Schaik et al., 2012)) and task fidelity (Vallance et al., 2015) provoke learners to associate their virtual experiences with later, real-world applications. Such a transfer of learning to unique situations enables learners to transfer knowledge, generalise concepts experienced in the virtual space, and develop social skills through their transboundary interactions.

Conclusion

Through involving students in real-world programming of robots and 3D printing of virtually created artifacts, theoretically-driven Constructionist virtual environments for effective learning have been created. The varied scenarios presented in this chapter have promoted designing, making and playing by learners in Japan, the UK and the USA. Given the results and interpretation of the data collected in these scenarios, it can be confidently reasoned that 3D virtual environments will bridgc the transboundary spaces for "new learning" in the 21st century. The next chapter extends this theme to game-based worlds as spaces of learning and making.

Acknowledgements

The research was funded by JAIST *kakenhi* 22650196 (2010-11) and 15K01080 (2015-17). Many thanks go to fellow researchers Dr. Stewart Martin, Hull University, UK; Catherine Namaani, University of South Wales, UK; Paul Wallace, Appalachian State University, USA; Malcolm Thomas and pupils at MACS South Wales, UK; Future University Hakodate students involved in the projects; Kenta Ibayashi (corktree18@ gmail.com); and Gabriel Campitelli (gabriel.campitelli@gmail.com) for his Unity programming expertise.

References

Anderson, L. W., Krathwohl, D. R., Airasian, P. W., Cruicshank, K. A., Mayer, R. E., Pintrich, P. R., Raths, J. and Wittrock, M. C. (2001) *A Taxonomy for Learning, Teaching and Assessing: A Revision of Bloom's Taxonomy of Educational Objectives.* New York: Longman.

Arnold, S. (2012) *Controlling Robots 6,000 Miles Away? No Problem*! National Instruments Developer Zone. Available at https://decibel.ni.com/content/groups/sweet-apps/blog/2012/03/15/ controlling-robots-6000-miles-away-no-problem.

Barker, S.B., and Ansorge, J. (2007) "Robotics as Means to Increase Achievement Scores in an Informal Learning Environment". *Journal of Research in Technology and Education*, 39(3): 229–43.

Catlin, D. and Blamires, M. (2010) "The Principles of Educational Robotic Applications (ERA): A Framework for Understanding and Developing Educational Robots and their Activities". In: Clayson, J. and Kalaš, I., eds. *Constructionism 2010: Constructionist Approaches to Creative Learning, Thinking and Education: Lessons for the 21st Century: Proceedings for Constructionism 2010: The 12th EuroLogo Conference*, 16–20 August, 2010 Paris, France.

Dede, C. (1996) "The Evolution of Distance Education: Emerging Technologies and Distributed Learning". *American Journal of Distance Education*, 10(2):4–36.

deFreitas, S. and Neumann, T. (2009) "The Use of 'Exploratory Learning' for Supporting Immersive Learning in Virtual Environments". *Computers and Education*, (52):343–52.

Dalgarno, B., Hedberg, J. and Harper, B. (2002) "The Contribution of 3D Environments to Conceptual Understanding". In O. J. McKerrow (eds.), *Winds of Change in the Sea of Learning: Proceedings of the 19th Annual Conference of the Australasian Society for Computers in*

Learning in Tertiary Education, 1:149–58). Auckland, New Zealand: UNITEC, Institute of Technology.

Kalantzis, M. and Cope, B. (2012) *New Learning: Elements of a Science of Education.* Cambridge, UK: Cambridge University Press.

Koenig, A., Iseli, M., Wainess, R. and Lee, J.J. (2013) "Assessment Methodology for Computer-Based Instructional Simulations". *Military Medicine*, 178, October Supplement.

Kolb, D. A. (1984) *Experiential Learning: Experience as the Source of Learning and Development.* Prentice-Hall: Englewood Cliffs, N.J.

Kress, G. R. (2003) *Literacy in the New Media Age.* USA: Routledge.

Papert, S. (1993) *Mindstorms. Children, Computers, and Powerful Ideas.* Basic Books: New York.

Papert, S. and Harel, I. (1993) *Constructionism.* USA: Ablex Publishing.

Piaget, J. (1972) "Intellectual Evolution from Adolescence to Adult". *Human Development*, 15: 1–12.

Schaik, P. van, Martin, S. and Vallance, M. (2012) "Measuring Flow Experience in an Immersive Virtual Environment for Collaborative Learning". *Journal of Computer Assisted Learning,* 28 (4):350–65.

Tarricone, P. (2011) *The Taxonomy of Metacognition.* New York: Psychology Press.

Thagard, P. (2005) *Mind: Introduction to Cognitive Science.* USA: MIT Press.

Vallance, M and Martin, S. (2012) "Assessment and Learning in the Virtual World: Tasks, Taxonomies and Teaching for Real". *Journal of Virtual Worlds Research*, 5(2):1–13.

Vallance, M., Naamani, C., Thomas, M. and Thomas, J. (2013) "Applied Information Science Research in a Virtual World Simulation to Support Robot Mediated Interaction Following the Fukushima Nuclear Disaster". *Communications in Information Science and Management Engineering (CISME)*, 3(5):222–32.

Vallance, M., Martin, S. and Naamani, C. (2015) "A Situation that We had Never Imagined: Post-Fukushima Virtual Collaborations for Determining Robot Task Metrics". *International Journal of Learning Technology*, 10(1):30–49.

Vallance, M. and Ibayashi, K. (2015) "Post-Fukushima 3D Virtual Collaboration and Communication for Active Learning". In *Proceedings of 5th European Immersive Education Summit*, 9-10 September 2015, Paris, France.

Vallance, M. and Towndrow, P. "Pedagogic Transformation, Student-Directed Design and Computational Thinking". *Pedagogies: an international journal* (In press).

Vygotsky, L. (1986) *Thought and Language.* MIT Press: Cambridge, MA.
Wiliam, D. (2011) *Embedded Formative Assessment.* USA: Solution Tree.

CHAPTER FOUR

MAKING KNOWLEDGE AND SURFACING INTUITION THROUGH A CITIZEN SCIENCE GAME

LADAN COCKSHUT

Introduction

In the preceding chapter, we learned how coding and making have been applied to transboundary contexts of learning. Continuing this theme of the global citizen, this chapter describes how these same dispositions can be applied to the democratisation afforded by citizen science.

In September 2011, scientists published news of a breakthrough. After a global effort comprising over a decade of trying – and failing – to generate a model for an enzyme-sniping protein critical in the reproduction of the AIDS virus, they had finally – after just three weeks of trying – been able to "generate models of sufficient quality for successful molecular replacement and subsequent structure determination" (Khitab et al. 2011, 1175). The refined structure provided new insights for the design of antiretroviral drugs in the treatment of the virus, they concluded. Whilst this was a welcome step toward additional treatments and a potential cure for HIV, the process by which this discovery was made was even more remarkable. Scientists had largely turned the work of protein folding (the process by which they would posit and generate models for structural determination) over to amateurs. Rather than bringing dozens of world-class professional researchers on board to solve this problem, the team (based at the Center for Game Science at the University of Washington) developed a citizen science game called Foldit and invited puzzle-solving gamers to try their hand at positing folded proteins. The game itself had a leader board and gamers could work in teams to solve the protein-folding puzzles. Most importantly, it tapped into areas of human-based computational skill that computer-based algorithms have yet to replicate or improve on: intuition, visual cognition and pattern-matching skills. As the authors noted, "The critical role of Foldit players in the solution … shows the power of online games to channel human intuition and three-dimensional pattern-matching skills to solve challenging scientific problems" (Khitab et al., 2011, 1177). Utilising a novel co-productive creative process designed around a citizen science game, this innovative approach to making knowledge enabled a significant step forward in an important area of scientific research. In the years following this breakthrough, a small but increasing number of citizen science-gaming approaches are being used in physical sciences research (Cooper et al. 2010; Trueille and Das 2014; Rallapalli et al. 2015) by enlisting large numbers of volunteers to analyse and produce data in immersive and creative gameplay environments.

Citizen science itself is not new but its gamification and digitisation are. Recent years have seen a noticeable upsurge in new forms of citizen science through the provision of shared data collection or analysis via digitisation (i.e., Zooniverse), collective knowledge creation within the online space (Wikipedia, Encyclopaedia of Life) and now the design of citizen science games: videogames created by scientists to engage and enlist the public (gamers) in scientific research and analysis (i.e., Foldit or EteRNA). These games provide a unique way of making knowledge between these two groups of participants: the scientist and gamer.

For almost as long as we have had digital games, there has been controversy about them. The pattern and emergence of these controversies are well reflected in the themes and trends in academic research and literature around the topic of digital games. While first seen as a technical marvel, or even a technique to verify or test computing, computer and video games were then largely ignored by academia until the late 1970s, or at least until their cultural popularity gained attention in the media. Suddenly, questions around their impact on social interaction and addiction and their causal relationship to violence and anti-social behaviours and norms were being raised. Their widespread popularity appeared to signal a shift in popular culture and generated new forms of playful engagement that early games and play theorists like Johan Huizinga and Roger Caillois could not have imagined when they wrote in the 1930s and '50s. (Huizinga 1938; Caillois 1958) And, as with many new things that are taken to by a noticeable part of society, they raise questions and expand possibilities.

A fellow games researcher asked me in late 2012 if I had seen these "citizen science games" that were starting to pop up. At that point I had only heard of Foldit and the sudden success its gamers had had in folding that AIDS-related protein (Khitab et al. 2011). For a researcher who had long been interested in studying the widening scope and capacity of games in society, this was exciting news. Here were scientists faced with a real challenge, one that could make a difference in studying and curing a devastating disease, and some unlikely allies had saved the day. It felt like the conclusion of a far-fetched natural disaster film where the unlikely hero swoops in at the eleventh hour and rescues the planet. These games, and their active facilitation of dialogue and creative making between what appears to be two unlikely allies, seem to demonstrate even more ways in which video games continue to evolve.

It seems fitting, then, that Brendan Koerner, in his *Wired* article about the citizen science game EteRNA, described it as a "science crowdsourcing tool disguised as entertainment" (2012). The games are designed with entertainment, competition and reward at their core to engage a widening group of participants and capitalise on their particular skillset: that of puzzle solving. These citizen science game pioneers have opted to shift the focus from eliciting the public's support using science alone to building in elements of gamification (Hamari, Koivisto & Sarsa 2014) to expand and sustain wider engagement and input. This chapter explores a selection of these games and considers the impact of drawing together what is often viewed as one the most laudable pursuits of our modern society, scientific research and analysis, with what is often seen as one of its more contentious elements, the video game. As with the commercially oriented video game, communities and supporters are forming around these games and signalling a new dynamic interaction between the professional and amateur, appearing to capitalise and hone in on specific skillsets of each group. This chapter, however, interrogates the opportunities and potential challenges that this relationship presents and considers questions around sustaining and designing these games going forward. Do games become something else when they can make knowledge? Are they reshaping the landscape of how scientific knowledge is produced, and who should and can be involved? Or are they simply symptomatic of our current digital era with its predilection to "gamify" everything?

Background

Contextualising the digital game

Why do we play games? Is it to entertain ourselves? To distract? To learn? To challenge? Play and games are concepts that seem interwoven into an associational relationship (called a bounded utility by games theorist Alexander Galloway [2006, 19]). Scholarly approaches to play and games across multiple disciplines have been predominantly situated within studies of leisure pursuits, animal behaviour or childhood development (Caillois 1958; Juul 1938; Smith 1984; Sutton-Smith 1986, 1997). In addition, within the humanities, the definition of play and games has typically been regarded through its meaning and utilisation within culture (Huizinga 1938). Play and games have also been considered in terms of a process of ordering or categorisation of rules and structure, particularly when attempting to define or contextualise them (Caillois 1958). Probably largely due to their pervasive nature, it is not surprising that play and games have been approached from different disciplines in different ways. This has been highlighted by some researchers, suggesting that making an over-arching theory about play is difficult. According to at least one play researcher, Brian Sutton-Smith, "when it comes to making theoretical statements about what play is, we fall into silliness" (1986, 1). He viewed that problems in conceptualising play come partly "because there are multiple kinds of play and multiple kinds of players" (1986, 6). Sutton-Smith attributes the complexity of defining play to its variability. He posits that play is a "facsimilization of the struggle for survival as this is broadly rendered by Darwin" (1986, 231). If, in fact, play represents the fundamental human drive to survive and all games "act out" that struggle, then play is more than just a trivial distraction or leisure pursuit. Play is not necessarily a tidy experience that always has a beginning, middle and end – there is dysfunction and obligation, there is the "work" of play, there is the failure in play.

Games theorist Jesper Juul draws on seven distinct (though not uncomplimentary) definitions of a game, all suggested by different academics (2005, 36), before suggesting a definition of his own.

> A game is a rule-based system with a variable and quantifiable outcome, where different outcomes are assigned different values, the player exerts effort in order to influence the outcome, the player feels emotionally attached to the outcome, and the consequences of the activity are negotiable.

The usefulness of Juul's definition is that it strips away any contemporary or historical factors that might limit an understanding of games whilst also considering the core elements of what makes a game work and how the nature of play (or the player) fits within that. But games and play are about more than simply rules or outcomes. They are also about action. The action or physical process of play connects the rules and outcomes of play with the components of such activity – such as through the digital interface or the game pieces – by which the player accesses and navigates the game. As Espen Aarseth (2001,1) explains

> Games are both object and process; they can't be read as texts or listened to as music, they must be played. Playing is integral, not coincidental like the appreciative reader or listener. The creative involvement is a necessary ingredient in the uses of games.

This making of play – the action of play – demands not only a "creative involvement" on the part of the player but also helps explain why games and play are so entwined with each other. As Aarseth suggests, unlike the appreciative music listener who can enjoy a great piece of music without actually having participated in its production, the player has an active role in making the game happen.

With regards to ways in which academic research has approached the study of the video game, this has often been in relation to its place within and impact on society. Some of the earliest studies into video games were interested in the health and psychological impacts of games on gamers. Research has looked at, in particular, the links between aggressive behaviour and violent games (e.g., Griffiths 1998; Ferguson 2010); addiction or pathological game use (King et al. 2009; Sim et al. 2012); the impact of digital games on childhood and adolescence (Olson 2010; Fromme 2011); and the gendered nature of games (Subrahmanyam and Greenfield 1994). Some studies, in response to some research, have engaged in a debate around whether there can be a valid categorisation of gaming as either addictive or aggression-inducing in nature (Wood 2008; Ferguson and Dyck 2012), suggesting that while academic research has been interested in discovering a link between games and their adverse impacts, successfully making a link (or disproving one) remains undetermined.

In addition to research into the psychological or sociological impacts of gaming, study into its health impacts has been more varied in scope, with some studies focused on the potential negative impacts on health such as the causal impact on obesity or attention deficit hyperactivity disorder (ADHD) (Burke et al. 2006; Chan and Rabonowitz 2006) while others have identified the benefits of gaming as a pain management tool (Raudenbusch 2003); in cognitive development or improvement among children or older adults (Basak et al. 2008; Whitlock et al. 2012); and as a benefit for individuals with neuropsychiatric disorders such as autism (Tanaka et al. 2010).

Studies into video games have also expanded to look at the nature of the games themselves (Aarseth 2001; Juul 2005); games design (Salen and

Zimmermann 2003); the narrative (Jørgensen 2010); and the relationship between the virtual "gaming world and the real world" (Galloway 2004, 1). Another way that interested scholars have reflected on the digital game is from the perspective of the interface (Galloway 2006, 2012) and the structure (from the devices through to the in-game) of the game (Ash 2009) and its related embodied actions. What the digital game was and how it could be studied and defined became a foremost interest as these scholars began to place their work in what was being referred to as (computer) games studies, an interdisciplinary field devoted to the digital game and its layers of meaning in action (Aarseth 2001) above their own individual disciplines.

New areas of research into the so-called "serious" or educational game, including, more recently, the citizen science game, have brought to the fore an interest in and attention to the use of gaming concepts and ideas in non-traditional, non-commercially oriented environments. Research into educational games has explored games developed to support education (often called "serious games") for use in the classroom (Prensky 2001, 2005); on the ways that existing forms of gamic action can support educational agendas to teach a particular subject or skills (Griffiths 2002; Lim 2009) or as an educational tool, particularly for students with disabilities (Khandaker 2009); and the links between gaming (particularly excessive gaming) and academic performance (Jaruratanasirikul et al. 2009). This has also led to recent attention around taking core game design ideas and related outcomes and applying them to other environments such as education, health or business through a process referred to as gamification (Reiners and Wood 2014; Surendeleg et al. 2014). Gamification is defined as "a process of enhancing services with (motivational) affordances in order to invoke gameful experiences and further behavioural outcomes" (Hamari, Koivisto and Sarsa 2014, 3026). Gamification is used primarily in contexts seen as being beyond actual conventional games. Hamari et al. frame gamification as being the "next generation method for marketing and customer engagement" (2014, 3025), and Deterding et al. (2011) have described it as a way to encourage positive user engagement in products and services. Gamification techniques rely predominantly on positive user feedback and tangible game-like goals (achievements, leaderboards, quests), and while there has been a growing interest in this approach within business, educational and third-sector areas, its effectiveness remains under-studied (Hamari et al. 2014).

All of these diverse areas of research and engagement, across disciplinary and thematic lines, suggest that the elements of play and games (and their impact) are finding their way into new environments and raising possibilities around their benefits, challenges and application beyond their traditional constructs. It is becoming clear that games and play are not merely a developmental construct of the young, nor simply a commercial venture. We should not be surprised when these principles of play and games find their way into the provision of academic research practices themselves. And as games are, at their core, an action-based medium, they seem to be a well-suited, malleable practice that allows for further modalities of engagement beyond the traditional or conventional.

Making citizen science into games

A few years ago, I informally asked a few science colleagues what they felt was limiting their discipline – what was needed to support the next great "leap forward" in their fields of research. Invariably a number of them said that greater computational power or innovations were required. Scientific research, one explained, requires increasingly sophisticated algorithmic innovations to effectively manage the increasingly massive data outputs that need to be analysed and handled. There are areas of research where human-based computing is acknowledged as still being ahead of any computational algorithm currently in place (Cooper et al. 2010; Eiben et al. 2012). Scientists working in these areas acknowledge that handling the analysis as a result of this era of big data requires innovating a "new approach to solving computationally-limited scientific problems" (Cooper et al. 2010, 756). And for some researchers and research projects, using a crowdsourced approach to scientific research which draws on an engaged public has proved an effective tool (Cooper et al. 2010; Treuille and Das 2014).

The modern professional scientist first emerged in the early 19th century – from the Scientific Revolution, which began in the 16th century – concurrently with the origins of the first doctorate degrees in the sciences. Even the term "scientist" in the English language is relatively new, having only been coined in the 19th century by William Whewell (Ross 1962). The doctorate in science was first established in Germany in the early 1800s and expanded to other nations in the late 19th and early 20th centuries (Rüegg 2004). Before this time, scientific research was largely conducted by individuals more typically referred to as natural philosophers, or scholars who had a philosophical interest in the natural or physical world. In these earlier days, the scholar who reflected on scientific ideas might also be considered a philosopher, and in some cases have taken orders from within the Church. An early scientist's qualification or predisposition to explore science was not necessarily related to a particular scientific qualification at university. According to modern standards, it could be argued that their work was, to a large extent, what might now be viewed as amateur.

Modern approaches to scientific research typically expect that it is performed by the trained, highly qualified professional. It has never fully abandoned the role played by the amateur, or citizen, however. As far back as the 18th century, volunteers have been sought on a large scale to submit or collect scientific information. Their input was particularly notable in areas of observation and data collection in the fields of biology, environmental science and astronomy (Dickinson and Bonney 2012). This form of citizen science relied on public engagement and the reliable submission of data to scientific societies or universities. As Dickinson and Bonney (2012, 1) state, "By our definition of citizen science as public participation in organised research efforts, hundreds of thousands of individuals around the world are "citizen scientists," people who have chosen to use their free time to engage in the scientific process".

Citizen science has grown by leaps and bounds in recent years, likely attributable to the expanding access to information technologies and the growth of grassroots advocacy, particularly in relation to environmental science. As Alan Irwin observed in the mid-1990s, citizens need to be active participants in science and the impact it has on the every day. He also argued that "science and technology should be seen above all as human activities" (2) and that "communities need to get involved" (105) in their activities. For Irwin, the nature of scientific citizenship was a dynamic one that characterised contemporary society (1995). This trend to advocacy through citizen science continued and expanded as Internet technology grew and scientists saw ways to not only educate but also engage large communities in supporting and learning about their research. Dickinson and Bonney see "large-scale citizen science as a microcosm of the changes that are occurring in science and society owing to the explosion of the Internet and the social web" (2012, 3). For some, the growing participation in citizen science "represents a fundamental change in the way that scientific work is distributed within society" (Good and Su 2013, 1931).

In environmental science, a lot of the literature exploring citizen science projects suggests that citizen science functions primarily to empower and encourage the public to increase their understanding of and support of science (Dickinson and Bonney 2012). Citizen science, it is argued, reaches and transforms the public. The projects on offer largely support this view, but ask for a limited engagement from the public around areas that pose less of a risk to the success of the project. The majority of citizen science games appear to avoid tasks seen as too complicated or skilled, such as data analysis or laboratory experimentations. Projects are mostly about data collection on a large scale: the public submitting a count of how many birds they have seen in their back garden (Audubon Bird Count), or through basic data analysis: counting images of penguins in Antarctica (PenguinWatch). Good and Su describe these forms of activity as encompassing "an emerging collection of approaches for harnessing such distributed human intelligence". They lament the lack of research and resources around the best ways to use these forms of human-powered engagements across various "scientific domains" (2013, 1925).

For many researchers, citizen science is a largely positive experience for the member of the public contributing to the scientific project: they are being educated and motivated to contribute to a greater good (Cockshut 2014). Many of the projects are highlighted and promoted for their ability to engage in public education or stewardship activities (BBC 2013, 2016). By engaging with citizen science, professional scientists can expand the culture of academic science beyond what is viewed as their primary markers of success, namely publications, teaching and the wider scientific community (Dickinson and Bonney 2012). That does not mean citizen science is not viewed by some as a risk to those key values; supporting and developing a cohort of citizen scientists can require resources and take time away from what is seen as core academic pursuits (Trueille and Das 2014). What remains less explored is the benefit these contributions can make for the scientists themselves, particularly beyond those key values that Dickson and Bonney refer to.

A good example of current citizen science or crowdsourced research projects are those housed on Zooniverse, an online portal to over forty different projects that the public can get involved in (accurate as of mid-2016). They include projects that go beyond science as well, covering the arts and humanities and the social sciences. Most of the projects involve visual cognition or data processing activities. In some citizen science projects, thousands of participants are credited with contributing to a project. In PenguinWatch 2.0 (in which citizen scientists are asked to classify penguins, chicks and eggs by pointing and clicking on their images), it is noted (as of June 2016) that almost 4 million images have been classified by over 36 thousand volunteers (PenguinWatch).

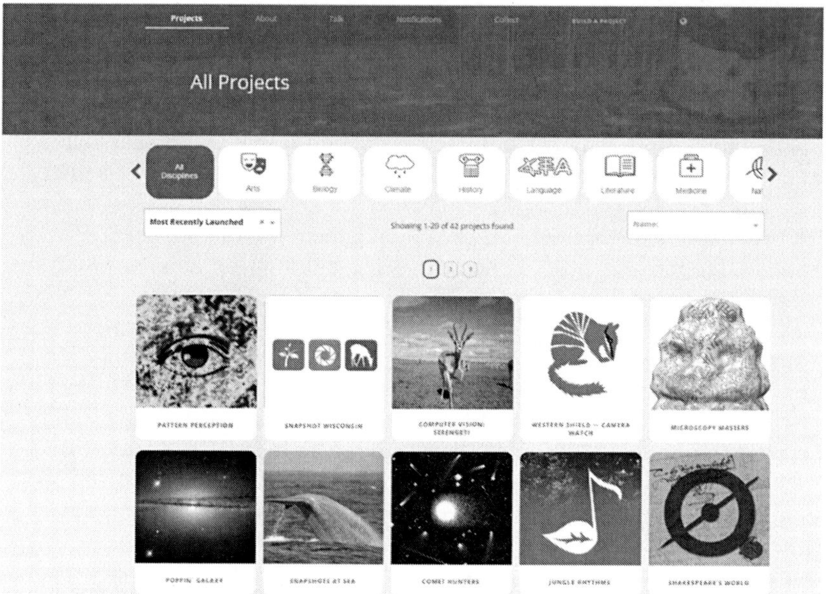

Figure 30 Screen capture of the Zooniverse citizen science portal (www.zooniverse.org), 2016

As academics are increasingly taking advantage of these new forms of digital and social web-related access through a range of citizen science projects, some have begun to think of new and alternative ways to tap into this large pool of potential volunteers to support their work and deal with the increasingly massive amounts of data that require processing and handling. In the case of a few of these scientists, some are using a game platform to engage their citizen scientists.

The earliest known example of a citizen science game, Foldit, was released in 2008. With data suggesting that video games are a primary leisure activity (ESA 2016), early proponents of using game platforms to facilitate certain large-scale research needs, Luis von Ahn and Laura Dabbish, advocated tapping into this time commitment to support research: "What if this time and energy were also channeled toward solving computational problems and training artificial intelligence (AI) algorithms?" (2008, 59). These games also wanted to tap into something else that citizen science was already doing: gather people to process with the massive output of data now characteristic of many scientific fields (Curtis 2014). Trueille and Das (2014, 507) also argue that using what they term a "massive open laboratory" through their game EteRNA is an effective way to mitigate the growing problems they see affecting the scientific method in an increasingly "big data" research environment.

> A growing spate of controversies, retractions, and fraud cases highlight the susceptibility of modern biology to untruths. Despite an elaborate peer review system, issues such as data manipulation, lack of reproducibility, lack of predictive tests, and cherry-picking among numerous unreported data occur frequently and, in some fields, may be pervasive. Some of these issues are further intensified by what is now a hallmark of modern biology, the use of high-throughput experimental techniques. ... In our view, however, hypothesis generation and experimental tests by creative scientists are what make science exciting and truthful. Therefore, 3 years ago we began to explore a new idea: rather than allow growing experimental data to overwhelm hypothesis generation, perhaps a larger number of people could be recruited to deeply analyze and design experiments. The result is what we term a massive open laboratory model for science.

In the case of EteRNA, this meant creating what may be seen as a fairly rudimentary puzzle game that taught the basics of RNA sequencing but established the gamers (or the citizen scientists) as an integral element of their overall laboratory strategy.

In the case of the game Fraxinus, the goal was a genomic study of the pathogen currently decimating ash trees in Europe, and designers utilised not only a puzzle-based casual game but released it on Facebook. The idea was to expedite the engagement of players in the problem due to the time-related pressure the researchers faced. The game, designed by Dan MacLean at Sainsbury Lab in the UK, was released within months of the first case of the disease being discovered in the east of England (Rallipalli et al. 2015). This approach drew on social media, game play and an urgent research need to propel its work forward.

For the creators of Foldit, its notable early protein-folding successes (Khitab et al. 2011) provided compelling early evidence in support of the hypothesis that using a large crowd of skilled puzzle- solving players could produce a result and be an effective tool for researchers.

> Although much attention has recently been given to the potential of crowdsourcing and game playing, this is the first instance that we are aware of in which online gamers solved a longstanding scientific problem. These results indicate the potential for integrating video games into the real-world scientific process: the ingenuity of game players is a formidable force that, if properly directed, can be used to solve a wide range of scientific problems. (1177)

But perhaps the most interesting aspect of this intersection of the gamer with the scientist is the notion of creative problem solving, or the shared making of knowledge, as stated by Trueille and Das (2014) in a preceding paragraph and also by Eiben et al. (2012) below.

> Crowdsourcing complex computational protein-design problems with a community of game-developed experts can be an effective way of creatively sampling the potential sequence space for the design of active-site loops that modulate enzyme activity. (192)

When citizen science meets the game

I recently sat with a group of my first-year undergraduate games design students to discuss citizen science games. These were predominantly male, aged 18–27, and self-proclaimed avid gamers used to blockbuster games like Fallout 4, Call of Duty, or World of Warcraft. These students were used to my challenging them to think beyond the typical scope of the commercially viable game and consider alternative games and their impact in other areas. I felt this was an important part of their learning process, particularly as they were fledgling game designers about to embark on a career in a field that has seen radical growth and shifts in its decades of existence, and that was still under development.

Most had never heard of citizen science games before, however. When I explained that these were games designed to help analyse actual scientific data using game platforms and puzzles, most were politely curious yet largely uninterested. "How is that even a game?" asked one of them. Another noted that they had heard of games like that but had presumed they were boring to play. A few were intrigued by the idea and discussed them in more detail. Perhaps, one posited, games like these might improve the negative perceptions of games and gamers. Another proposed that introducing more games like this in school could make certain subjects more interesting to learn. This inevitably segued to some students arguing that a lot of so-called "serious" or educational games were poor quality and that students only played them in school as it was better than working out maths problems on a worksheet. I asked them if they would feel better about playing a game if they knew it was supporting a greater aim or answering important questions. A number of them agreed, but a few remained ambivalent. "Games are meant to be fun", one remarked. "It doesn't really matter what kind of data they are built on or if playing it helps in some other way – it just has to be fun to play". "And if it wasn't fun", I asked, "but you still knew it was helping with research?" "Then", he responded, "I probably wouldn't really bother to play it really.

At least not for long". To me, this *ad hoc* conversation with my students raised a few interesting questions around the nature of games and whether or not a citizen science game – a game which may be more about purpose than simply fun – has not only a role for the creative making of knowledge but could also be regarded as part of the canon of video games.

As discussed earlier in this chapter, there are increasing examples of games being used in non-entertainment contexts, including serious or educational games, gamification in business or health and now the emerging genre of citizen science games. While academic research has been interested in studying a range of ways games and play are impacting modern society, there is less work being done around the interactive dynamic between the scientist and gamer in the citizen science game. Based on my own work looking at the experience of play in a massive multiplayer online role-playing game (MMO) (Cockshut 2012), I was interested in how these fledgling citizen science games might compare to the genuinely global, massive for-entertainment games, particularly in relation to their community relations and approach to game-making. In the summer of 2014, I conducted a limited online ethnographic study of a small selection of citizen science games. I was primarily interested in the experiences of players and scientists around their motivations for creating meaning (scientist) and making knowledge (gamer) through such a game and how it might more effectively support research and public engagement going forward. To inform this initial study, I used publicly available online forum discussions, anonymised online communications with participants, and academic journal articles and media reports to draw insight.

Research conducted online is no longer viewed as a new phenomenon; it has become established as a valid form (and source) of investigative enquiry (Lee et al. 2008). The work of Christine Hine (2000) and Annette Markham (1998; 2009) are considered seminal contributions to thinking through the methodological and ethical problematics of online research. A holistic approach to designing online-based research can be found, particularly in Hine's work on researching the Internet in 2000. As Hine writes, "An ethnography of, in, and through the Internet can be conceived of as an adaptive and wholeheartedly partial approach which draws on connection rather than location in defining its object" (2000 10). I have utilised this adaptive and connective approach in my own study of online persistent game environments and their complexities as expressed through the actions of play, community building and competition (Cockshut 2012). This approach was supported through the work of Fields and Kafai (2010) when they applied this idea of a "connective ethnography" (drawn from Hine's earlier work, among others) to trace gamer practices across the "different spaces" of play (2000, 91). The notion of effective connective online ethnography requires engaging with various tools and techniques to pull data together. Taylor describes her research practice as "bricolage, pulling from a variety of techniques, tools, and methods to understand a mix of practices, representations, structures, rhetoric, and technologies" (2006, 17). I found echoing a similar approach to Taylor's to be effective in my own ethnographic work in these first-generation citizen science games, particularly in relation to adapting and modifying my research collection methodology around the needs and practices of the players themselves.

My preliminary small-scale study of these games and their creators (scientists) and knowledge makers (players) was interested in the following:

1. Drawing out which values mattered to each group and what sustained their contributions to (gamers) or development of (scientists) these types of games; and
2. Learning the nature of any communities that had developed around these games and how those relations were being sustained.

The aim of this work was to conduct a preliminary scoping study to inform potential social-science-related research in and around player experiences in citizen science games. While the data generated from this study represents a small sample and should not be viewed as conclusive, they do provide some interesting areas which warrant further study.

About the citizen science game

For the purposes of this preliminary work, three citizen science games were studied: EteRNA, Foldit and Fraxinus. Each of them built a game platform around a specific set of data that can be analysed and handled better using human-based computational skills. As one scientist described it, their game was designed to take advantage of "using the crowd as a human super computer". All of the games are designed to be accessible, free to play and understandable to a non-scientist. While Fraxinus is accessible as a Facebook-hosted game (Rallapalli et al. 2015), the other two have dedicated websites with forums and information.

Of those players interviewed for this preliminary study, I observed that while the majority had little previous engagement with mainstream commercial videogames, some had had experience playing casual or puzzle-based games. I also noted that some had a computing or science-related background, though most did not. And among the two web-based games studied, I found that there were active engaged communities of players who had formed subgroups and other forms of communication and interaction to support their activities. This had also expanded to creative forms of engagement and knowledge-making between scientist and player through the game.

In the following two sections, all of the comments and communication with scientists and players have been anonymised, unless previously published elsewhere (via the media, the game sites or academic journals or publications). I spoke with players in two different citizen science games and with scientists associated with three different games.

The scientist as creator

In this section, I highlight certain core values that emerged from conversations with and comments by scientists involved in designing and managing citizen science games.

Value 1: Has a computing-based problem which needs human insight and intuition

Perhaps the most telling motivation for scientists to adopt a new approach like crowdsourcing research is when a limitation is reached in their own research approach. When David Baker and his colleagues ran into such difficulties, they innovated a method which eventually expanded into a citizen science project – Rosetta@home – in 2005. And from this project eventually emerged the Foldit game.

> To enable the more comprehensive searching necessary to find the low-energy native energy minimum, we decided to enlist the help of the general public. We created a distributed computing project called Rosetta@home … in which volunteers donate spare cycles on their computers to carry out folding trajectories. (Baker 2014, 225)

For some, the human ability to spot patterns and make intuitive leaps is key to the citizen science game. In the case of EteRNA, Rhiju Das acknowledges that while computing programs try to decipher and build new strands of RNA, none could match the human ability to pick up on subtle emerging patterns (Gross 2012) to effectively predict new ones. "We're relying on humans to do something computers can't do, which is create hypotheses," Das said. "There's no computer that can do that. They don't have imaginations" (Das in Gross 2012). And for Das, the decision to make his citizen science project into a game was due to, he says, certain qualities that make online gaming fun.

> The most addictive online experiences, they have certain qualities that are game-like. … They're social. You have a chat. You feel like you're in there with some other people and it also has to give you a huge amount of positive feedback. (Das in Gross 2012)

Value 2: Has a lot of data and needs a lot of resources

In discussions with one scientist, Das explained part of the driving force behind creating a citizen science game was having "a lot of data to churn through" that needed processing, and that the approach was deemed necessary in order to speed up the design and to "create a pool of volunteers who could scale human-generated experimental design and analysis along with biochemistry's rapidly expanding experimental throughput."

Value 3: Is not afraid to be imaginative and take risks

A number of researchers have pointed to how their disciplinary background pushes them to try new things; the majority interviewed were from a bioinformatician background (a relatively new interdisciplinary scientific field of research that brings together computing, mathematics, statistics and engineering to study biological sciences). "We [bioinformaticians] like to try new approaches and aren't intimidated by the mechanics of processing and taking in data this way," one explained to me.

For some, the potential output is worth the risk of using a game to support research even when segments of the scientific community may not yet fully embrace the idea.

> At the beginning, we weren't sure this approach would work, which is why we set the game up to be continually changing and improving. I think initially there was some 'naysaying', but hopefully through some of [its] successes of [the game], as well as other games that involve the public in scientific research, that has changed.

Value 4: Appreciates the value of skilled players

At least two of the researchers behind one of these games had a direct experience with gaming, which likely contributed to their openness to using game platforms to support areas of research (Das and Trueille 2012;

2014). For other researchers, the unique contribution that players make to the process has been invaluable.

> The "skills of top players far outweighs anything I could have imagined." (Adrien Trueille in Gross 2012)

> FoldIt players in the last 2 years have made a number of quite important contributions: they solved the structure of a retroviral protease, developed new algorithms for finding low energy protein conformations and improved a de novo designed enzyme by rather large-scale redesign of the active site. (Baker 2012)

For the scientist as creator, the values of innovation, risk-taking and resourcefulness are relevant and their need for support enables them to work with and value a skilled non-scientist community.

The player as knowledge maker

Without the player, the citizen science game cannot achieve its potential: making the knowledge that supports or innovates the wider research aims of the project. In this section, I highlight what players value whilst playing and making knowledge in citizen science games.

Value 1: Mutual respect and scientist engagement

For the players, a tone of a shared responsibility and ownership is expressed and enacted through the goals of the game. As one player said, "Our game, our scientists, and we are their players. This is a joint adventure."

Value 2: Emotional investment and community involvement

For many of those interviewed, an emotional investment and attachment to the game was expressed: "I really love the idea with citizen science. I feel the term describes well what I am. I'm a citizen doing science… my feeling … is empowerment. We play, fail and succeed." Another player discussed the impact that the community has had on their emotional investment and commitment to the game.

> I think the reason that I'm so emotionally invested … is because of how much I have gotten out of it. I've made friends and I've gotten the chance to be part of something that not everyone can be a part of. I also found a lab to work at due to my involvement in [the game]. [It] has helped to shape

> my life in a multitude of ways, and I guess that's why it means so much to me.

The shared sense of involvement was expressed by yet another player, particularly by referencing their own work using the plural pronoun: "We all help and contribute. But we do so differently. We try make up for the weaknesses and for what is lacking."

Value 3: Contributions and work

Markers of contribution can be self-determined or encouraged through the game itself. Work and contributions were important to many of the players I chatted with. Terms like problem solving, "work", and "help" suggest an active productive engagement with the game. "The way I see it, the faster we get the new players level up, the more we can all contribute to science. We have problems to solve." For another player, the association with a greater aim through playing a citizen science game was unmistakable: "I work for something."

And for yet another player, there was the idea of not only actively supporting the project ("help the protein") but also the notion that they could develop and hone new skills and abilities through playing the game: "I want to help the protein be what it should be ... I like to measure myself against something ... I get to use abilities that I didn't know I had".

For the players of these citizen science games, the result of this sample set of interviews suggests that they valued not only a sense of mutual engagement and respect but also favoured the opportunity to contribute meaningfully to both the activity and community of their respective games. The process of gameplay is not merely about the outcomes of the game but also about the contributions and emotional investment that players make.

Reflecting on citizen science games: challenges and possibilities

It seems clear that citizen science games signal an interesting opportunity for both the scientist and game player to collaborate and make new areas of knowledge together. Such games not only enable the non-scientist to contribute meaningfully to timely research but to do so in a way that could generate more concerted and regular interactions between these two seemingly disparate groups of people. There appear great potentialities for community building, empowerment and outcome-based commitments to surround these efforts and to sustain long-term engagement. However, recollecting my own informal discussion with some of my game design students, it is a challenge to draw enough mainstream players to what may be misconceived as a boring or "serious" game, and having a significantly large group of skilled gamers is critical to making a suitable dent in the huge volume of data that require analysis (Gross 2012).

Coupled with this is the academic cynicism that may greet projects of this type. For one of the scientists involved, the cynicism may relate to different backgrounds and training.

> A lot of bench-based scientists don't make the mental leaps about how distribution of a problem and highly parallel consideration can help; it isn't in their training to go from a reductionist philosophy to seeing how large-scale involvement could work.

For some, the problems of perception within the academic community pose a genuine risk to the scientists who engage in these types of projects.

> The major current barrier may … be the career risks that these projects pose for their creators. In particular, videogames, which appear critical for recruiting scientifically engaged citizens, are generally viewed as incompatible with "serious" or rigorous research. (Trueille and Das 2014, 508)

This suggests that producing or supporting citizen science games as a legitimate research platform could be punitively reacted to in some quarters, which could hinder the willingness of some to innovate in these areas.

Another academic viewed the cynicism as fading when these games successfully make research discoveries.

> I think initially there was some "naysaying", but hopefully through some of the successes of [our game], as well as other games that involve the public in scientific research, that has changed.… Hopefully we are contributing to the view that gaming isn't wasteful and can be a legitimate way to do science.

Another area of concern, which a few players interviewed raised, relates to ethical issues surrounding games of this sort. One concern related to players being encouraged to volunteer excessive hours in support of the project: "I recalling (sp.) watching a … video with one of the researchers speaking, a while back. He was boasting about getting players to play for 24 hours in a row. And I thought to myself, this is irresponsible." Another added this thought: "Scientists are sometimes blind to the side effects [of excessive playing] as they often don't play the game or follow chat". Being mindful of the ethics and dynamics at work in this type of maker dynamic may require further consideration or study into the expectations placed on players.

As with any new endeavour, particularly one that puts together scientists who may not ordinarily work with or manage large communities of volunteers with players who are clearly passionate about supporting their games, a great deal can be learned about what does and does not work. A good indication of this has been how these games continue to expand and grow, such as Foldit now developing Nanocraft and, more recently, EteRNA's expansion into research involving tuberculosis. Not all games remain active, however, such as in the case of Fraxinus, which stopped collecting data in 2015 (Rallapalli et al. 2015).

Probably one of the more exciting possibilities relating to where citizen science games could go and their potentially transformative impact on research and community building is in the recent adaptions and modifications made at the EteRNA game site. EteRNA's origins as an RNA building game is seeing cross-disciplinary applications beyond RNA alone. In 2016, it launched an endeavour to support developing diagnostic kits for tuberculosis, which can be used at home and in developing nations where access to conventional diagnostic approaches are typically far more limited (EteRNA, 2016). Scientists appear not only to have made improvements but are branching into a new area of research – that of optimising the EteRNA community to branch into an area where their puzzle- solving potentialities are particularly useful by identifying RNA combinations that could help build a basic, home-use tuberculosis diagnostic kit aimed at the developing world – and aiming to build on not only what is well established by engaging with their most loyal and supportive gamers but also by providing a key goal (or quest, if one wishes to use a game design-related term).

Directly addressing the EteRNA players and prospective players in a promotional video uploaded on the game's site, Rhiju Das, the project's principal investigator, outlined the game's new direction for players.

> To help us get ready to target tuberculosis we have made two major updates to the EteRNA project: first, veteran players and developers have created a new, beautiful set of puzzles so within a couple days of play you will not only understand the basics of RNA design, but the tools and feedback you'll get; second, we've completely expanded the experimental throughput of EteRNA. Now, every month, if you can get us one million molecules, we can synthesize all of them and process them through the supercomputer and get them back to you. We hope that you'll join us and if

we succeed, your designs and your puzzle solving strategies will have an actual impact on the future of medicine.

Conclusion

This exploration of the citizen science game – which brings together two very different groups to collaborate – highlights an innovative example of what making knowledge can look like in novel applications. It is already showing promising signs of being an effective tool (Khitab et al. 2011). As with other areas impacted by video games, crowdsourcing and gamification, it appears that citizen science games demonstrate an emerging field which could have a potentially significant impact on other areas of academic research. While the player is critical to the success of a game of this nature, the engagement of the scientific team behind it is just as important.

As Star and Griesemer noted in their work looking at early 20th-century examples of citizen scientists and professional scientists collaborating, "Scientific work is heterogeneous, requiring many different actors and viewpoints. It also requires cooperation" (1989, 387). It would seem that this cooperative element is what is critical to the success of these citizen science games. This is manifested through sustained regular contact between scientist and player, meaningful ways to make and develop contributions (as well enunciated through EteRNA's commitment to not only update its game but also engage closely with committed players) and even employing participatory methods going forward when designing a new game. All of these require consideration when developing games of this nature, particularly when so much is at stake for the scientists involved.

Another consideration worthy of further research is the fact that these games could represent a new type of research methodology, one which could be considered not only in relation to games for the physical sciences but also in social sciences or humanities. Whilst this preliminary study suggests that communities can and do build around citizen science games in much the same way as commercial games, it is also clear that how these communities form are unique to the "citizen science" aspect of the process and that this requires further study and consideration going forward. If, as Trueille and Das (2014, 507) note, "creative scientists are what make science exciting and truthful", then surely working closely with the intuitive, imaginative gamer can only support and promote these important areas of work going forward. In the next chapter, these themes of the learning of science, and intuitions, are elaborated upon.

Acknowledgements

This preliminary study was completed during the summer of 2014 through the kind input of colleagues and players who participated in informal online and email interviews and discussions with me about their experiences with a citizen science game. I wish to thank our editor, Kenneth Lim (National Institute of Education, Singapore), for not only championing the publication of this work but also for facilitating and chairing our maker culture seminar at the 2014 Royal Geographic Society conference, which brought all of us together around such an innovative and interesting topic.

References

Aarseth, E. (2001) "Computer Game Studies: Year One [Editorial]". *Game Studies* 1 (1). http://www.gamestudies.org/0101/editorial.html. Last accessed June 2, 2016.

Ash, J. (2009) "Emerging Spatialities of the Screen: Video Games and the Reconfiguration of Spatial Awareness". *Environment and Planning A* 41:2105–24.

Baker, D. (2014) "Protein Folding, Structure Prediction and Design." *Biochem. Soc. Trans.* 42: 225–29.

Basak, C. et al. (2008) "Can Training in a Real-time Strategy Video Game Attenuate Cognitive Decline in Older Adults?" *Psychol. Aging*.

BBC. (2013) "Citizen Science 'harnesses power of public'". http://www.bbc.co.uk/news/science-environment-24532308. Last accessed June 2, 2016.

Burke, V., Beilin, L.J., Durkin, K., Stritzke, W.G., Houghton, S., and Cameron, C.A. (2006) "Television, Computer Use, Physical Activity, Diet and Fatness in Australian Adolescents". *Int. J. Pediatr. Obes.* 1(4): 248–55.

Caillois, R. (1958). *Man, Play and Games*. Champaign/Urbana, Illinois: University of Illinois Press.

Chan, P.A., and Rabinowitz, T. (2006) "A Cross-sectional Analysis of Video Games and Attention Deficit Hyperactivity Disorder Symptoms in Adolescents". *Annals of General Psychiatry* 5: 16.

Clarke, C.C. (2013) *Be the Change: Saving the World with Citizen Science*. Amazon Publications.

Cockshut, L. (2012) *The Way We Play: Exploring the Specifics of Formation, Action and Competition in Digital Gameplay among World of Warcraft Raiders*. Durham Theses, Durham University. Available at

Durham E-Theses Online: http://etheses.dur.ac.uk/5931/. Last accessed June 3, 2016.

—. (2014) "Addictive Online Games Make Citizen Science a Hit". *The Conversation.* https://theconversation.com/addictive-online-games-make-citizen-science-a-hit-30552. Last accessed June 2, 2016.

Cooper, S., Khatib, F., Treuille, A., Barbero, J., Lee, J., Beenen, M., Leaver-Fay, A., Baker, D., Popović, Z., and Foldit players. (2010) "Predicting Protein Structures with a Multiplayer Online Game". *Nature* 446:756–60.

Curtis, V. (2014) "Online Citizen Science Games: Opportunities for the Biological Sciences". *Applied & Translational Genomics* 3(4): 90–94.

Deterding, S., Dixon D., Khaled, R. and Nacke, L. (2011) "From Game Design Elements to Gamefulness: Defining Gamification". In *Proceedings of the 15th International Academic MindTrek Conference: Envisioning Future Media Environments*, September 28-30, Tampere, Finland, ACM: 9–15.

Dickinson, J.L. and Bonney, R. (2012) *Citizen Science: Public Participation in Environmental Research*. Ithaca, NY: Cornell University Press.

Eiben, C.B., Siegel, J.B., Jacob B. Bale, Seth Cooper, Firas Khatib, Betty W Shen, Foldit Players, Barry L. Stoddard, Zoran Popovic & David Baker. (2012) "Increased Diels-Alderase Activity through Backbone Remodeling Guided by Foldit Players". *Nature Biotechnology* 30:190–92.

Electronic Software Association. (2016) "Essential Facts About the Computer and Video Game Industry".
http://essentialfacts.theesa.com/Essential-Facts-2016.pdf.
Last accessed June 2, 2016.

Ferguson, C.J. (2010) "Blazing Angels or Resident Evil? Can Violent Video Games Be a Force for Good?" *Review of General Psychology* 14(2):68–81.

Ferguson, C.J., and Dyck, D. (2012) "Paradigm Change in Aggression Research: The Time has Come to Retire the General Aggression Model". *Aggression and Violent Behavior* 17(3):220–28.

Fields, D.A. and Kafai, Y.B. (2010) "Knowing and Throwing Mudballs, Hearts, Pies, and Flowers: A Connective Ethnography of Gaming Practices". *Games and Culture* 5(1):88–115.

Fromme, J. (2011) "Computer Games as a Part of Children's Culture". *Game Studies* 3(1).

Galloway, A. (2004) "Social Realism in Gaming". *Game Studies* 4(1).

—. (2006) *Gaming: Essays on Algorithmic Culture.* Minneapolis: University of Minnesota Press.

—. (2012) *The Interface Effect*. Cambridge: Polity Press.

Gill, V. (2016) "Penguin Watch: Public Asked to Aid Antarctic Research". *BBC News*. http://www.bbc.co.uk/news/science-environment-35981212. Last accessed June 2, 2016.

Good, B.M. and Su, A.I. (2013) "Crowdsourcing for Bioinformatics". *Bioinformatics* 29 (16): 1925–33.

Gross, D. (2012) "Turning Gamers into Citizen Scientists". *CNN Gaming Reality*. http://edition.cnn.com/interactive/2012/08/tech/gaming.series/research.html. Last accessed June 4, 2016.

Griffiths M.D. (1998) "Violent Video Games and Aggression: A Review of the Literature". *Aggression and Violent Behavior* 4: 202–13.

Griffiths, M. (2002) "The Educational Benefits of Videogames". *Education and Health* 20(3):47–51.

Hamari, J., Koivisto, J. & Sarsa, H. (2014) "Does Gamification Work? A Literature Review of Empirical Studies on Gamification". In *Proceedings of the Annual Hawaii International Conference on System Sciences*. IEEE Computer Society: 3025–34.

Hine, C. (2000) *Virtual Ethnography*. London: Sage.

Huizinga, J. (1938) *Homo Ludens: Study of the Play Element in Culture*. London: Routledge. (Originally published in German.)

Irwin, A. (1995) *Citizen Science: A Study of People, Expertise and Sustainable Development*. London: Routledge.

Jaruratanasirikul, S., Wongwaitaweewong, K., and Sangsupawanich, P. (2009) "Electronic Game Play and School Performance of Adolescents in Southern Thailand". *CyberPsychology & Behavior* 12(5).

Jørgensen, K. (2010) "Game Characters as Narrative Devices. A Comparative Analysis of Dragon Age: Origins and Mass Effect 2". *Eludamos. Journal for Computer Game Culture* 4 (2):315–31.

Józsa, G. I. G.; Garrett, M. A.; Oosterloo, T. A.; Rampadarath, H.; Paragi, Z.; van Arkel, H.; Lintott, C.; Keel, W. C.; Schawinski, K.; Edmondson, E. "Revealing Hanny's Voorwerp: Radio Observations of IC 2497". *Astronomy and Astrophysics* 500(2): L33–L36.

Juul, J. (2005) *Half-Real: Video Games between Real Rules and Fictional Worlds*. Cambridge, MA: MIT Press.

Khandaker, M. (2009) "Designing Affective Video Games to Support the Social Emotional Development of Teenagers with Autism Spectrum Disorders". *Stud. Health Technol. Inform*. 144: 37–39.

Khatib, F., DiMaio, F., Foldit Contenders Group, Foldit Void Crushers Group, Seth Cooper, Maciej Kazmierczyk, Miroslaw Gilski, Szymon

Krzywda, Helena Zabranska, Iva Pichova, James Thompson, Mariusz Jaskolski and David Baker. (2011) "Crystal Structure of a Monomeric Retroviral Protease Solved by Protein Folding Game Players". *Nature Structural and Molecular Biology* 18: 1175–77.

King, D., Delfabbro, P., & Griffiths, M. (2009) "The Psychological Study of Video Game Players: Methodological Challenges and Practical Advice". *Int. J. Ment. Health Addiction* 7: pp. 555–562.

Koernier, B. (2012) "New Videogame Lets Amateur Researchers Mess with RNA". *Wired*. http://www.wired.com/2012/07/ff_rnagame/. Last accessed June 3, 2016.

Lee, R.M., Fielding, N., and Blank, G. (2008) "The Internet as a Research Medium". In Fielding, N. (ed.) *The Sage Handbook of Online Research Methods*. London: Sage, pp. 3–20.

Lim, K. Y. T. (2009) "The Six Learnings of Second Life: A Framework for Designing Curricular Interventions In-World". *Journal of Virtual World Research* 2(1).

Markham, A. (1998) *Life Online: Researching Real Experience in Virtual Space*. Walnut Creek, CA: AltaMira Press.

—. (2009) "How can Qualitative Researchers Produce Work that is Meaningful across Time, Space, and Culture?" In Markham, A., and Baym, N. (eds), *Internet Inquiry: Dialogue among Scholars*. Thousand Oaks, CA: Sage.

Olson, C.K. (2010) "Children's Motivations for Video Game Play in the Context of Normal Development". *Review of General Psychology* 14 (2): 180–87.

Oskin, B. (2012) "Teens and Video Games: How Much Is Too Much?" *LiveScience*. http://www.livescience.com/22281-teens-video-games-health-risks.html. Last accessed June 2, 2016.

Prensky, M. (2001). *Digital Game-based Learning*. New York: McGraw-Hill.

—. (2005). "Computer Games and Learning: Digital Game-based Learning". In J. Raessens & J. Goldstein (eds.), *Handbook of Computer Game Studies*. Cambridge: MIT Press.

Rallapalli, G., Fraxinus Players, Saunders, D.G.O., Yoshida, K., Edwards, A., Lugo, C.A., Collin, S., Clavijo, B., Corpas, M., Swarbreck, D., Clark, M., Downie, J.A., Kamoun, S., Team Cooper, MacLean, D. (2015) "Cutting Edge: Lessons from Fraxinus, A Crowd-sourced Citizen Science Game in Genomics". *eLife* 4: e07460. https://elifesciences.org/content/4/e07460/article-info. Last accessed June 4, 2016.

Raudenbusch, B. (2003). “Study Suggests Link Between Video Games and Pain Relief”. Wheeling Jesuit University NewsRelease. http://www.wju.edu/about/adm_news_story.asp?iNewsID=769&strBack=%2Fabout%2Fadm_news_archive.asp.

Reiners, T. and Wood, L.C. (2014) *Gamification in Education and Business*. Heidelberg: Springer.

Ross, S. (1962) “Scientist: The Story of a Word”. *Annals of Science* 18(2): 65–85.

Rüegg, Walter. (2004) *A History of the University in Europe: Volume 3, Universities in the Nineteenth and Early Twentieth Centuries (1800–1945)*. Cambridge University Press.

Salen, K. and Zimmerman, E. (2003) *Rules of Play: Game Design Fundamentals*. Cambridge: The MIT Press.

Sim, T., Gentile, D.A., Bricolo, F., Serpelloni, G., and Gulamoydeen, F. (2012) “A Conceptual Review of Research on the Pathological Use of Computers, Video Games, and the Internet”. *International Journal of Mental Health Addiction* 10 (5): 748–69.

Smith, Peter, ed. (1984) *Play in Animals and Humans*. Oxford: Blackwell.

Star, S.L., and Griesemer, J.R. (1989) “Institutional Ecology, ‘“Translations” and Boundary Objects: Amateurs and Professionals in Berkeley's Museum of Vertebrate Zoology, 1907–39”. *Social Studies of Science* 19: 387–420.

Subrahmanyam K., and Greenfield, P. (1994) “Effect of Video Game Practice on Spatial Skills in Girls and Boys”. *Journal of Applied Developmental Psychology* 15:13–32.

Sullivan, B. et al. (2009). “eBird: A Citizen-based Bird Observation Network in the Biological Sciences”. *Biological Conservation* 142: 2282–92.

Surendeleg, G. et al., (2014) “The Role of Gamification in Education – A Literature Review”. *Contemporary Engineering Sciences* 7(29–32):1609–16.

Sutton-Smith, B. (1986) *Toys as Culture*. New York: Gardner.

—. (1997). *The Ambiguity of Play*. Cambridge, Mass.: Harvard University Press.

Tanaka, J.W., Wolf J.M., Klaiman C, Koenig K., Cockburn J., Herlihy L., Brown C., Stahl S., Kaiser M.D., Schultz R.T. (2010) “Using Computerized Games to Teach Face Recognition Skills to Children with Autism Spectrum Disorder: The Let's Face It! Program”. *J. Child Psychol. Psychiatry* 51(8): 944–52.

Taylor, T.L. (2006) *Play Between Worlds: Exploring Online Game Culture*. Cambridge, MA: MIT Press.

Trueille, A. and Das, R. (2014) "Scientific Rigour through Videogames". *Trends in Biochemical Sciences* 39(11): 507–09.

von Ahn, L., Maurer, B., McMillen, C., Abraham, D., Blum, M. (2008) "reCAPTCHA: Human-Based Character: Recognition via Web Security Measures". *Science* 32: 1465–68.

von Ahn L., and Dabbish, L. (2008) "Designing Games with a Purpose". *Communications of the ACM* 51(8): 58–68.

Whitlock, L.A., Collins McLaughlin, A., and Allaire, J.C. (2012) "Individual Differences in Response to Cognitive Training: Using a Multi-modal, Attentionally Demanding Game-based Intervention for Older Adults". *Computers in Human Behavior* 28(4):1091–96.

Wood, R.T.A. (2008) "Problems with the Concept of Video Game "Addiction": Some Case Study Examples". *International Journal of Mental Health Addiction* 6:169–78.

Web sites and games referenced

Audubon BirdCount (http://www.audubon.org/conservation/science/christmas-bird-count)

Call of Duty (Activision/Aspyr Media, 2003)

Civilization (Microprose, 1991)

EteRNA (http://www.eternagame.org/web/)

Fallout 4 (Bethesda Softworks, 2015)

Foldit (http://fold.it/portal/)

Fraxinus (https://www.facebook.com/fraxinusgame)

PenguinWatch (https://www.penguinwatch.org/?_ga=1.82446302.970630001.1464787366#/)

World of Warcraft (Blizzard Entertainment, 2004)

Zooniverse (https://www.zooniverse.org/)

CHAPTER FIVE

JOURNEYS IN THE MAKING: SUPPORTING THINKERING THROUGH MAKER MOTES

KENNETH Y T LIM

Introduction

The increasingly participatory culture of learning – described in the preceding chapter – that characterises so much learning in authentic contexts outside of the formal spatial and temporal bounds of schooling is exemplified in maker culture. Such movements recognise that understanding is socially constructed. With regards to design thinking, there is an increasing recognition – since Hagel's *et al* (2008) seminal paper in the Harvard Business Review – that these dispositions and sets of expertise are of critical value to ensuring the nimbleness and adaptivity of societies in the 21st century. This is in large part because disciplinary domains are less accurately described as "stocks" of knowledge and more accurately as "flows" in an age of the networked learner. In such a characterisation, learners are adopting much more co-equal stances with more traditional domain arbiters as they participate and negotiate in the de- and re-construction of knowledge and the ontologies thereof. The learnings that accrue from defining ourselves as social beings – in relation to social others – are very different from those arising from an understanding of self as a standalone construct: the latter reinforces a notion of the acquisition of knowledge as stock; the former foregrounds an understanding of the negotiation of knowledge as flow.

In such performative environments, the traditionally binary distinctions between success and failure are rendered meaningless because learners realise for themselves that they are not only seeking a continuously shifting bar but – critically – have some influence over the nature of the bar itself. That is to say, learners realise for themselves they have the ability to create their own contexts for personally meaningful experiences of learning.

Learners engage in the creation and curation of contexts through deliberate participation in play. By "play" we refer not only to situations in which the learners are actively participating in the structured activities of games but also to the dispositional approach of the learner to attempting to understand whatever is presently holding his/her attention as a system to be analysed, de- and reconstructed (either/or metaphorically and/or literally). Play is therefore an extremely intentional activity (Huizinga 1955), and also a disposition which is increasingly defined in negotiation with one's social others.

Framing learning through the disposition of play is important because it has the corollary that "failure" (as traditionally defined) is an option – to the extent that it is understood as a learning opportunity. Personal worth is understood as a developmental process ("flow"), as in "I am getting better at this"/"I am understanding better how this works".

There is a growing awareness among science educators of the need to de-emphasise the memorising of de-contextualised scientific facts and place greater emphasis on science in the everyday world, and developing deep understanding through inquiry-based learning (Singer, Marx and Krajcik 2000). The relatively multi-disciplinary nature of environmental science (together with its values orientation) makes it an ideal candidate for a science, technology, engineering and mathematics (STEM)-based curriculum design. Designing curriculum around STEM is often predicated upon finding tasks which are meaningful and authentic to students. Traditionally, however, data presented to students is often abstract, decontextualised and presented in forms which presume relatively high numeracy and graphicacy among students. Thus, for example, conventional weather data is complicated by the microclimate of the built environment, especially of urban heat island effects. As students typically have no access to a mesh of data points, nor the means to observe concomitant weather phenomena, the cause-and-effect reasoning is usually abstract and far removed from the experience of daily lives.

Since 2013, the present author and his team of researchers from the National Institute of Education in Singapore have been working on the use of a network of low-cost, open-source unobtrusive environmental sensors placed throughout a school campus. Through this network, teachers have the wherewithal to design curriculum which would permit and encourage the interrogation of real-world microclimatic data from within an environment already familiar to the students, so that their intuitions about local environmental factors and systemic relationships – which would otherwise have remained tacit – might be surfaced and dialogued upon in collaboration with their peers and teachers.

Such a multi-disciplinary approach to curriculum design helps learners develop their graphicacy and data literacy in authentic ways (the "M" in STEM). Using datasets derived in real time from their own school campus, learners are potentially able to interrogate the data in ways which would be contextualised to their own local knowledge of their school (the "S" in STEM). The datasets are generated from a wireless mesh of remotely connected sensors placed around the school campus, potentially at sites determined – at least in part – by the learners themselves (the "T" in STEM). In turn, the sensors are designed and assembled using readily available open-source hardware and software, such as the Raspberry Pi and Arduino (the "E" in STEM).

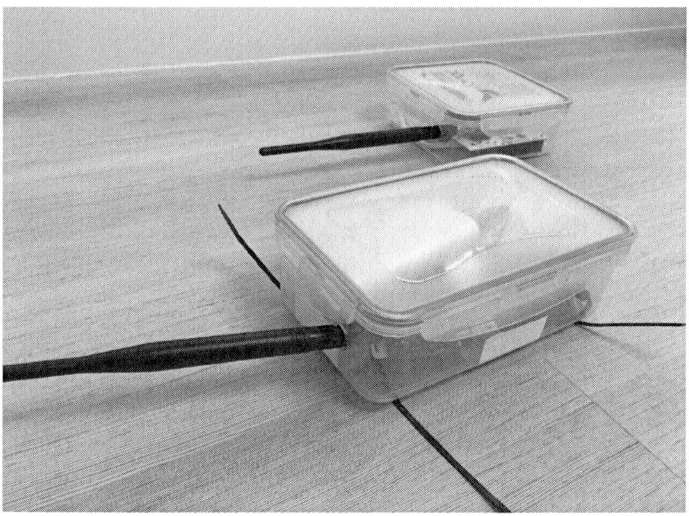

Figure 31 Low-cost environmental sensor and hub

With their own sensor mesh and a means to visualise the data, we believe students will be better able to "talk" through these datasets to surface their intuitions, confront them, and develop means to move from nascent forms to more expert forms of knowledge.

Review of literature

Kong (Kong et al., 1979; Kong, 2000) has argued that children and adolescents in highly-urbanised Singapore view nature as something which is orderly and well-maintained. She continues that this rather limited perception arises from the fact that nature is

> a "waste of time". All the teenage members of the school group acknowledged that nature was not very much a part of their consciousness. When bored and thinking about places to visit and what things to do, the tendency was not to think of activities associated with nature. When thoughts about the natural world did surface in their minds, it was often in the context of school work, for example, their geography lessons, during which nature was more about conceptual issues and scientific processes than everyday environments of potential fun and enjoyment. (Kong et al. 1999,3)

Kong's observations are important because it is our considered position that such "everyday environments of potential fun and enjoyment" constitute the substrate upon which intuitions about geography – intuitions about the nature of the man-land relationship – are formed and developed. Such intuitions, in turn, shape geographical ways of knowing, and are thus critical to informing how novice geographers (such as students in school) approach and understand the world.

One of the seminal researchers on children's conceptions about weather phenomena is Henriques (2002). Her review of the literature was initiated on the basis that relatively few studies had been carried out to understand what children think about topics in the earth sciences. One of her most salient findings is that while weather is ostensibly a topic within the earth sciences, many of the misconceptions students held regarding weather originated from the natural sciences; examples included properties of water, and phase changes and the water cycle. Her often-cited cautionary conclusion was that "in many cases, students' misconceptions are not addressed in the curriculum, allowing them to exist unchallenged".

Some of the studies Henriques unearthed in her review were Sere's (1985) and that of Driver, Squires, Rushworth and Wood-Robinson (1994). These just served to highlight particular misconceptions which students held – for example, that air has weight was challenging even for high school students (Sere 1985), and that air exerts pressure only when it is moving downwards (Driver et al. 1994). With regards to humidity, Bar (1989) commented on the difficulty children have in understanding air as a "permanent substance", and how this – in turn – led to what Russell and Watt (1990) observed was the difficulty that fifth-graders had in identifying air as the final location of evaporating water. Lee, Eichinger, Anderson, Berkheimer and Blakeslee (1993) built on this preceding work to suggest that such difficulties of understanding persist into students' middle-school years. Likewise, when Aron et al. (1994) conducted a study on participants ranging from pre-service teachers and students of various ages (from middle-school to college) on topics such as air pressure, humidity and cloud composition, their conclusion was that across all age levels, people did not understand weather concepts.

This alarming pattern of results arising from research into children's understanding of natural weather events has continued beyond Henriques's study and into the early 21st century. In their 2008 study on middle-school and college students' conceptions about extreme weather events and hazards, Polito, Tanner and Monteverdi came to the rather damning conclusion that while

> conceptual research in science education has advanced during the past fifty years… conceptual research in meteorology is clearly lacking… for example, there are apparently no research articles about alternative conceptions of weather in the Journal of Geoscience Education, the main publication for educational research in the geosciences.

Notwithstanding the preceding, Rappaport did publish a paper of relevance to this chapter in that same journal a year later. Echoing Henriques's original critique, he first remarked that "little exists in the literature to specifically address how students understand weather, particularly at the secondary and undergraduate levels". Insightfully, he went on to say that

> along with formal instruction, young people possess a lifetime of observational experience with the water cycle. They have all seen kettles boiling, bathtubs steaming, and the accumulation of clouds in the sky before a rainstorm… to the instructor, this suite of common examples represents a windfall of opportunity. Any classroom with a window and a thermometer may become a laboratory for the discussion of weather.

Critically, though, Rappaport ended this rosy promise with the lament that "personal experience suggests that these connections are not being made in many classrooms. Consequently, undergraduates are unable to connect theories with actual phenomena".

One particular study is noteworthy in the context of this chapter, not only because of its possible cultural affinities to local contexts (the study was conducted with third-graders in Taiwan) but also because it investigated pictorial representations of data regarding a natural hazard (in the case of the Taiwanese study, not of haze but of typhoons). Thus, Ku, Ho, Peng and Tsai (2012) concluded that when children were presented with weather data, they tended to focus more on the pictorial representation rather than the textual information; critically – in the context of this chapter – they also cautioned that it could not be ignored that "charts might also result in alternative conceptions and negative effects".

Such an approach echoes Ben-zvi-Assaraf's (2005) observations that students in a "broad, context-based, unit" on the water cycle showed a "distinct improvement" in their ability to form mental models of complex processes, and were "better able" to identify and anticipate relationships.

The conceptual framework undergirding this part of the chapter is therefore that – at least with respect to the relationship between humans and the natural environment, and the way this relationship is approached in the formal curriculum – alignment between the assessment of children and their day-to-day lived experience is critical to developing an enduring understanding beyond rudimentary textbook recitation. This framework is broadly described by the present author's work in Disciplinary Intuitions, which is elaborated upon in Lim (2015). We suggest that an overlooked element of this alignment is the role that intuitions about geography play in shaping such understanding, and how these intuitions can sometimes be very powerful in lensing understanding either accurately or inaccurately. The challenge – from the point of view of curriculum designers (who are, by definition, disciplinary experts) – is in reminding ourselves of just how subliminal some of these day-to-day lived experiences might be.

Experience-based learning can be a powerful approach to pedagogy. Central to/compatible with the rationale of experiential learning is the belief that the use of concrete representation of the objects/ concepts being learned leads to better outcomes. Scientific Visualization (SciV) is one such method that helps concretise the learning process. SciV refers to the creation and use of "dramatic scientific images and their animation" to aid in the process of scientific inquiry, and/or to help make classroom learning a more authentic experience (Gordin and Pea 1995).

By linking the abstract qualities of weather (e.g., humidity and temperature) to easily intelligible visual representation, students are able to analyse data in a manner consistent with the principles advocated for experiential learning. Gordin and Pea (1995, 261) outline the ways in which scientific visualisation can help science education:

> 1) making a scientific view of the world more accessible; 2) providing a means for authentic inquiry; 3) empowering students with tools they can

use in a wide variety of fields; 4) laying groundwork to enable students to understand and critique scientific policy.

Indeed, empirical studies/reports have shown the advantages of using SciV in classroom settings. The ChemViz project (Koker and Rowe 1993) utilised SciV for the teaching of atomic interactions, and it was found that students became more motivated and were able to increase access to difficult scientific concepts. Another project, the IPT project, likewise introduced the idea of teaching science through image processing. The approach was able to encourage a teaching style of active inquiry and produced significant increase in student motivation, especially for the underrepresented and at-risk student groups (Greenberg 1992; Greenberg, Kolvoord, Magisos, Strom and Croft 1993).

It would be appropriate at this juncture to reflect upon an existing technology – Geographic Information Systems (GIS) – its impact, and to imagine a place for it in a school curriculum. The use, definition and capabilities of GIS are so broad that there is no clear short definition. A general generic description may be: a geographic information system is an organised collection of computer hardware and software, people and infrastructure that makes possible the acquisition and storage of geographic and related attribute data for the purpose of retrieval, analysis and display to promote understanding and assist decision making (ArcGIS, 4).

For the past decade, every weather program, news report, newspaper and map, including popular applications such as Google Maps, has stream-and-compile information from the local area. Educators have also recognised the promise of GIS as a technology to support learning through inquiry across various social and natural sciences (digital geo, 77). However locally, this technology is not widely considered, and the percentage of teachers who have received training and then go on to implement lesson plans in the classroom is very small. The goal of letting students use GIS to engage in something approaching authentic inquiry is rarely realised.

One reason GIS has not achieved either the broad use or the kind of use many have hoped for is that educators have access to GIS tools that were already in the commercial market. Many of these tools are developed for other uses and context, and require training on the part of the teachers and the students. The customisation of GIS tools for educational use has been limited, firstly, by cost, and, secondly, by vendor reluctance to produce low-cost alternatives to their software.

To summarise, the present author and his team have designed a curriculum model to support the setting up of real-time environmental sensors and linking them to a 3D virtual world creating unique GIS tools for novice users in school environments. The spatial contextualisation afforded by the representation of data within a virtual rendition of the school campus would reduce the learners' cognitive load (Sweller 1988). Our interest in the application of GIS is not strictly textbook or test-driven, although we expect positive impact on the school curriculum. Our goal is to use these tools to support inquiry and investigation into the environment, through data analysis and data visualisation, in the classroom.

Piloting the study in Singapore

The methodological design described was an exploratory study in which environmental datasets generated in real time by a networked mesh of open-source sensors would help students and community members learn environmental science and promote their understanding about their local environment. The study was piloted in a school in Singapore.

The present author and his team subsequently added the affordance to the data architecture of superimposing data from the sensors into a virtual representation of a school campus. Dubbed "Maker Motes" (a pun on "Make a Mote"), this network consists of an open-source electronics platform (Arduino), which is a small battery-powered computer connected to a set of various sensors. The final device is able to collect the following data: air pressure, noise levels, ambient light, humidity, pressure and air quality. In terms of installation, each sensor is fixed to a particular location (e.g., a pillar or wall) and can then be left to run autonomously (only needing to have its battery replaced and recharged periodically).

In terms of data transmission, each sensor mote sends the sensor readings wirelessly to a low-cost, open-source hub device (Raspberry Pi) at a customisable rate that provides users with a rich, meaningful set of data (e.g., every half an hour or every hour, as determined by the user). The sensors can be placed at different locations of the campus. Combining the rich data generated by the network of sensors and the virtual representation of a school campus (again on an open-source platform – OpenSim), one would be able to generate 3-dimensional representations of various environmental factors such as temperature, air pressure, humidity, light, noise and air quality.

Teachers can use the tools to make general statements more specific, and also let students learn to look closer at the data. For example, a student may comment that it only rains in the afternoon for the past month based on his experience. A teacher can point out that the data also suggest rains at night, so the student statement is a good description of his experience but not necessarily true.

Figure 32 Placing a self-contained low-cost environmental sensor

Every day we ask questions with geographical and spatial components. Students may already have a lot of tacit information and data of their immediate day-to-day environment, but often have difficulty describing it with precision and clarity. A local data collecting network can help them make accurate observation of data patterns, and also seeing subtle variations in those patterns. The present system can help the forming and investigation of hypotheses on the environment. Specifically, it helps the students to develop the ability to conduct and monitor investigations of the local environment, and verify the data against hypotheses. Students can use the data as evidence for an argument, and move from observing a pattern to developing a geographical claim. For example: "the temperatures in various areas of the school rise sharply around 10am and level off in the afternoon, dropping after 4pm. Based on this data pattern, it is best not to have outdoor lessons between noon and 3pm."

Typically, an intervention would begin with a workshop for students, to introduce them to the sensors and the various environmental variables that might be measured. During this initial workshop, students would have access to the open-source hardware, and be given at least an hour to go through an orientation activity. They would also have the benefit of having mentor-figures (teachers or members of the research team) on hand. After this initial workshop, it is envisaged that most of the lessons will be held during curriculum time in regular classrooms. A possible lesson framework might be:

- Inquire – Thinking about your environment, turning your observation into a hypothesis
- Acquire resources – Identifying the information and data needed to test your question
- Explore data – Turning collected data into maps, tables and graphs and looking for patterns
- Analyse the data – Drawing valid conclusions from the data
- Act – Thinking about how to share this knowledge and use it to improve your environment

A possible scenario of how such a lesson might unfold over time might be: a teacher says to the class, "It's been pretty hazy these few days. Which part of the school do you think has the worst quality of air?" "What about the most humid part of school?" "What about the shadiest?" "When?" "Why?"

By responding to these (and similar) questions, the students would surface their intuitions (valid and/or invalid) about factors influencing their local microclimate.

The problem this study attempts to address is that schools do not generally have a functional weather station within their premises; consequently, the line of inquiry ends with the students responding to the teacher's first round of questions. For schools with a functional set of weather instruments, the inquiry could potentially continue with the teacher saying, "Now that we have got your responses, let's see what we can do to verify your hypotheses". However, even then, the result would be a pointilistic description of data from the weather instruments, which would be limited in both temporal as well as spatial coverage (this is because weather instruments are expensive, schools have limited sets, and teachers do not have the luxury of time to get the students to take readings over an extended period of time because of the opportunity costs).

Such representations of data suffer from a further problem; namely, that the graphs and charts would be difficult to meaningfully interpret because they would have been decontextualised into only two dimensions (i.e., the microclimatic variable over time) – the role of space as a context underpinning the variable would have been stripped out.

The study addressed these limitations through the combination of open-source sensors measuring various aspects of environmental quality with a scale-rendition of the school compound in an open-source immersive digital environment. Because of the relatively low-cost of the sensors, we will eventually be able to cover the school compound with a much finer mesh – over both space and time – of data loggers than the pointilistic and opportunistic method of having students take readings only during a limited duration of (say) their science lesson.

Just as significantly, one is able to put the context back into learning (Hung, Lee and Lim 2012) by retaining the spatiality of the datasets by plotting them in their actual positions using the immersive model of the school's campus – this allows the students to interrogate the data with respect to topography, intervisibility, time of day, solar incidence, etc. (all being factors which would not otherwise be able to be represented using traditional Cartesian graphs).

Gee (2003) wrote about the role of what he has termed Projective Identity in game-based learning. Briefly, Gee describes how – in well-designed learning environments – a learner might potentially develop a projective identity as an amalgam which complements both his or her atomic (human) identity and the virtual (avatar) identity, and how such projective identities might persist beyond the instantiations of the game and/or the immersive environment to influence values and behaviours in other (non-game) contexts. Gee's thesis thus speaks directly toward the present framing of intuitions as developed through the lived experience, which can therefore include embodied experience in both human- and avatar-based settings. For example, the diagram below illustrates how variables might be represented within an immersive environment in terms of colour, shape, diameter of base, height and translucency. In turn, these multiple dimensions are contextualised according to the environment's topography, taking into account other influencing variables such as the time of day and solar incidence (note the shadows).

The data visualisation is not a 2D map but a 3D virtual environment. The environment itself is a familiar one to the students – their own school. The environmental data are collected in real time in the actual real-world environment so the students would have first-person embodied experiences of these data and also enough tacit information to make observations and predictions of data patterns. Compared with the conventional methods, virtual spaces provide students with a psychologically safe learning environment within which they can participate in experiential learning, practice skills, try out "what if" hypothetical scenarios and make mistakes without serious repercussions.

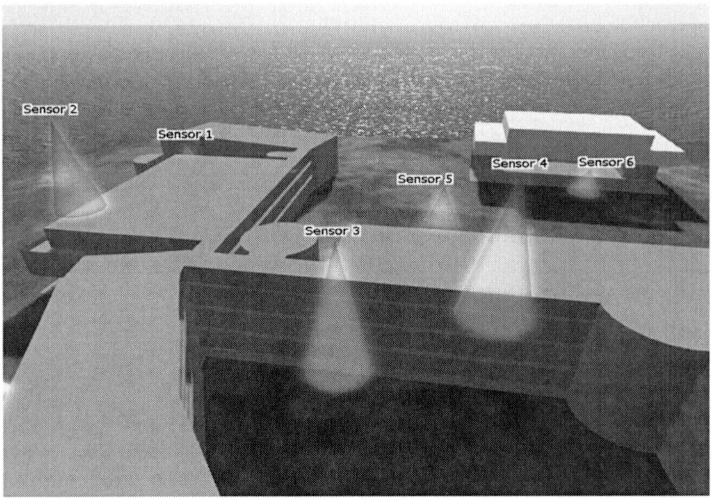

Figure 33 Example of how the intervention lends rich spatial context to environmental data

Taking the curricular approach to contexts of learning in Indonesia

This approach to learning can easily be adapted to rural contexts as the sensors do not require an existing electrical infrastructure. They are wholly self-contained and self-assembled. In such a scenario, the sensors would help farmers and villagers have a clearer understanding of how the microclimate within their settlement varies, and will thus allow them to make better planning decisions (e.g., in terms of irrigation).

In March 2016, the project was extended to five schools in the Bandung /Lembang area of Java, Indonesia. Two criteria were employed in the choice of schools. The first was urban /peri-urban setting and the second was altitudinal variation. Specifically, urban schools have better access to supporting facilities in the learning of science and STEM than their peri-urban counterparts. Sites were also chosen on the basis of their altitudinal variation and situation along the slopes of the volcano Tangkuban Perahu (the southern foothills, where the settlements of Bandung and Lembang are located). The schools were sited between 890 metres and 1245 metres above sea level. This would allow for a greater variation in microclimatic variables such as temperature and air pressure.

Participants are junior high school students (year 7 and year 8). Students from the inner city school represent children who have better access to technology while students from rural schools have only limited access to technology.

The design is sufficiently robust to accommodate interruptions in the schools' wireless communication infrastructure. The photograph below illustrates teachers from the various schools discovering how they can access the real-time data from the sensors through their own handhelds.

Figure 34 Teachers having hands-on experience with Maker Motes

The present system also overcomes the key challenges (Tan, Hedberg, Koh and Seah 2006) of using traditional data loggers. Our sensors are designed to collect real-time data and transmit it to a server. Therefore, there is no set-up time or logistics activities in the classroom, and class time can be devolved to learning activities. The data can be compiled beforehand by the teachers and can be represented in a variety of forms – paper-based and digital. If desired, there need not be any direct handling of sensors equipment by the students, thereby avoiding any equipment malfunctions due to mishandling.

In terms of ease of scaling and sustainability, the virtual environment is highly customisable, and features a scripting language that allows data to be read from and exported to a variety of commonly used databases, including cloud-based services (e.g., Dropbox) and productivity suites (e.g., Microsoft Office). Any design changes or improvements can be easily implemented. For example, the system will be able to reflect changes in the physical environment (e.g., new school structures, upgrading, etc.). Sensor positions can be changed easily both physically and in the virtual environment, which means the teachers can customise their learning activities. The teachers and students can also redesign the visualisation model to better represent the data they have collected. Scaling up can easily be achieved because both hardware and software are open-source and low-cost. The sensors are battery-powered and have proven to be waterproof even in tropical thunderstorms. If necessary, they can also be connected to solar kits.

Finally, the datasets might also be used in a proactive manner by staff and students to conceptualise and design measures to improve the quality of the school environment, such as in terms of noise, shade and air quality. Through the study, we are therefore able to design learning environments which provide students and teachers with boundary objects (in the form of time-series data represented over a three-dimensional space and over time) which could subsequently be discussed as students seek to verify their intuitions against the empirical data generated by the fine mesh of open-source sensors monitoring the school's local environmental quality.

Taking Maker Motes further through crowdsourcing

The opportunity to take Maker Motes further presents itself in two related dimensions. First, there has been an increasing momentum behind incorporating elements of STEM in both formal and after-school learning settings. However, the push toward learning with STEM has largely been limited to "making for the sake of making" and/or "building circuits for the sake of building circuits". That is to say, learners and the general public have not been presented with ways for taking what they have designed and built forward beyond the immediate context of the activity itself.

The second dimension of the opportunity is that government agencies and non-government organisations (NGOs) may lack local, contextual and timely data with which to make decisions; this is particularly the case with respect to – for example – the incidence of diseases such as dengue fever, patterns of bird migration, and other instances which impact the social good.

Low-cost open-source environmental sensors can now be potentially put into everybody's hands and homes. These sensors upload data from their local environment to a data set that government agencies and NGOs can use for their decision making. This data set is big, has inherent spatial information in it, and is updated in real time.

From another perspective, since the data generated by the environmental sensors is being used for the social good, it gives meaning and authenticity to the learning tasks that the purchasers of the sensors engage in through, say, an online curriculum.

The potential impact would be aligned with the Infocomm Development Authority's (IDA) vision of Singapore as a Smart Nation. This is because the crowdsourcing of the motes represents the building of a data infrastructure which government agencies (e.g., the Singapore Civil Defence Force (SCDF), the Health Promotion Board (HPB), the National Environment Agency (NEA)) and third parties (e.g., the Nature Society (Singapore)) could mine for localised and timely information which will make their decision making more robust. Significantly, there is also a potential export impact as the model can be adopted by other countries and regions, such as Australia and California, and can be applied to (for example) wildfire management.

As described earlier, there are two complementary areas-to-be-addressed to the innovation (namely STEM for STEM's sake, and a lack of local timely data for government agencies and NGOs to make decisions). The entire innovation – including the two dimensions – is depicted in the following diagram.

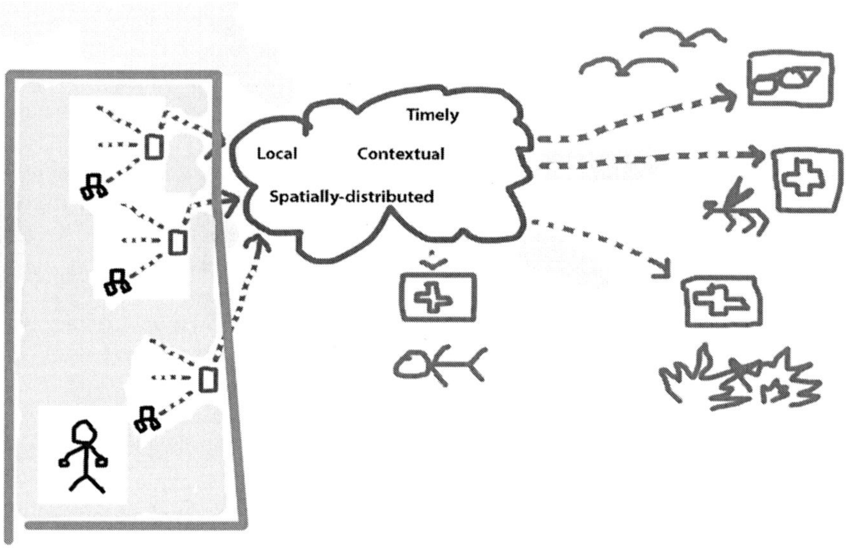

Figure 35A Overview of crowdsourced potential of Maker Motes

As depicted, the innovation has several elements. First, a distribution model needs to help people get their hands on (either pre-built or self-assembled) low-cost open-source electronic components (such as Arduino and Raspberry Pi). The assembly and application of these components could be supported through a subscription-based model to an online curriculum. Through this curriculum (and as they "play with" the environmental sensors which they assemble from their constituent parts), the general public will learn about (a) concepts in STEM and electronics, and (b) their local environment (their microclimate). This part of the innovation is depicted in the following diagram.

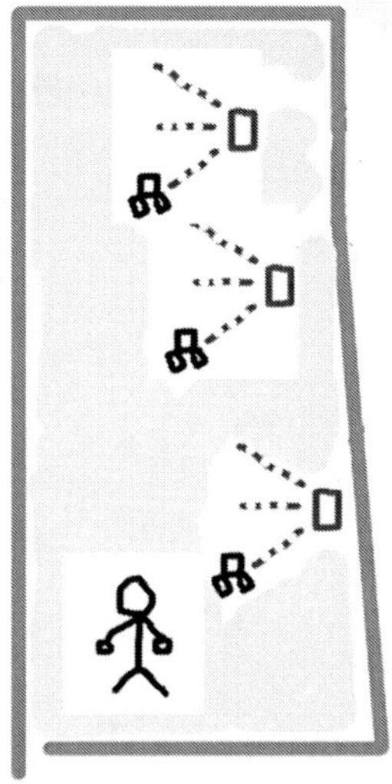

Figure 35B Framing of the curriculum within a crowdsourced model

A second element of the innovation is the big data generated by the spatially distributed Maker Motes. This is represented by the following diagram.

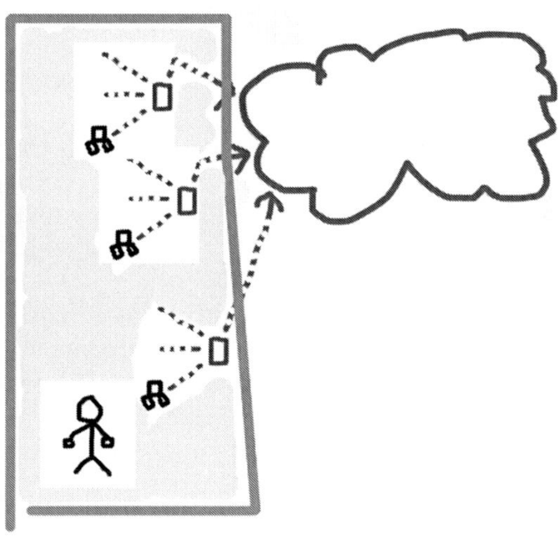

Figure 35C Crowd-based data sourcing in the cloud

The final major element of the innovation is the mining of the big data by government agencies, NGOs and other third parties through bespoke data-analytic dashboards and / or licensable APIs. This is represented in the following diagram.

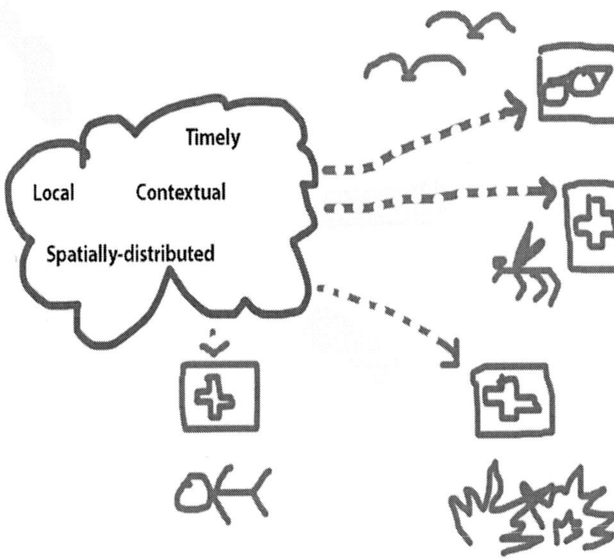

Figure 35D Maker Motes for the wider social good

Because the data is local, contextual, spatially-rich and timely, such third parties will be able to make more informed decisions and more optimal use of their limited resources. With respect to usage cases in Singapore, possible NGOs would be:

- Health Promotion Board (HPB) / National Environment Agency (NEA) and dengue incidence, related to microclimatic variables
- Singapore Civil Defence Force (SCDF) and emergency calls regarding heatstroke and asthma, related to microclimatic variables
- Nature Society (Singapore) and sightings of migratory birds, related to microclimatic variables

The innovation could also be exported to regions and countries (such as California and Australia) that experience wildfires because variables such as temperature and humidity might be incorporated into the crowdsourced GIS.

As such, the two primary areas of novelty are – first, the use of hyperlocal crowdsourced data obtained through open-source self-assembled sensors for the greater societal good; which in turn provides a high degree of authenticity and meaning to the learning about STEM and electronics; and second, government agencies, NGOs and other third parties will have access to local and timely data from a crowdsourced data infrastructure that they would not otherwise have access to, and can mine this data to optimise their resource-utilisation.

Concluding remarks

There are currently many sites and initiatives targeting the introduction of STEM learning to students all over the world. These tend to fall within one of two learning formats; on the one hand, online STEM resources tend to offer resources and lesson plans that facilitate actual classroom or project activities for educators or learners. A second learning format is represented by the Arduino resource sites, which tend to be online tutorials with a clear learning goal for each lesson. Similarities between the two formats include the use of animations, videos, pdfs and sample codes, which makes engaging in the activities easier. Some of them also have social networking elements with a forum where users can post their projects and share comments and messages.

A fusion of the two types of learning formats would lead to a new platform for online learning: a structured series of lessons based on a working project that cater to the online learning community, which is delivered partially or entirely through the internet. Such a learning environment would consist of a holistic environment involving student learning, peer synergy and academic knowledge. The collaborative communication in such an online virtual learning environment would permit students to communicate without having to physically talk or engage with one another, and would allow all parties to have an equal opportunity to communicate their knowledge

In order to minimise the barriers for implementing a successful online STEM program, programs need an effective and efficient online course design. The approach taken would need to consider curriculum and standards as well as academic rigour. STEM learning and the need to create an engaging curriculum with a range of metacognitive and content-specific instructional support should be present. The courses should include systems thinking, creativity, collaboration and communication.

Online course instructors need not only to have a strong understanding of their content area but also an appreciation for how technology affects the content and pedagogy of what they are trying to teach.

Viewed from this framework, while there may be prior initiatives and examples of each of the component parts of the learning system (e.g., prior art in makerspaces, construction kits and so forth), to the best of our knowledge there are few ecosystems that synthesise these various elements into a pedagogically coherent whole similar to the one described in this chapter.

Thus, for example, while the National Research Foundation in Singapore started a three-year project known as the National Science Experiment in 2015 – in which around 30,000 students in Singapore were given data loggers with which to collect environmental data – the key problem was that the data was not directed toward investigation or inquiry; instead, it was akin to the collection of data for its own sake. This was similar to moves toward gamification or the uninformed transference of concepts from the game industry to wider learning activities.

To elaborate, the economics of the gaming ecosystem tend to reward developers who can make games that are fast, cheap and briefly very addicting before users inevitably move on to the next trifle. When crafting a game designed to teach learners how to solve algebra equations effectively – something that likely requires a significant amount of pedagogical research – treating the development of educational games the same way as ones designed solely for entertainment suddenly becomes fairly problematic.

The problem with developing such a piece of software to be used for training/learning is that the development process can be long and resource-intensive, restricted to limited use cases, and adoption can be slow. Because the curriculum we envisage would be in support of attempts to inform more effective decision making of real-world problems (such as the incidence of dengue, bird migration patterns and health problems among the general population, as described in preceding examples), not only would the learning tasks for the children be more authentic but also there could potentially be a high impact on government agencies and NGOs with access to the data generated from the Maker Motes.

The application of game design techniques and virtual environments to non-game contexts, such as business, education and social impact, challenges is gaining traction. Companies use these techniques and technology for productivity enhancement, training, team building and innovation. Governments, non-profits and educational institutions are also applying these techniques. The mechanics and theories of design and immersive environment can certainly be applied to create engaging experiences within and without these environments.

However, enduring understanding and learning require a thoughtful deliberation of pedagogy, learning theories and motivational psychology, as well as sensitivity to the limitations and invalid assumptions of the affordances of these methods and technologies. A better and holistic understanding of learning pedagogy and learners' intuition would shape the application and design of learning, training and knowledge sharing in organisations and society at large. In this way, our approach is aligned with current impetuses to develop entrepreneurial dispositions, such as through encouraging a tolerance for uncertainty. The final chapter of this book attempts to synthesise these strands into the beginnings of a theory of maker education.

Acknowledgments

It is with deep gratitude that the author would like to acknowledge that funding for the intervention study in Indonesia described in this grant comes from a Digital Learning for Development (DL4D) grant, administered by the Foundation for Information Technology Education and Development (FIT-ED) of the Philippines, as part of a program jointly funded by the International Development Research Centre (IDRC) of Canada and the Department for International Development (DFID) of the United Kingdom

References

Ben-zvi-Assaraf, O. (2005) "The Development of System Thinking Skills in the Context of Earth System Education". *Journal of Research in Science Teaching*, 42(5):147–58.

Gee, J. (2003) *What Video Games Have to Teach Us about Learning and Literacy*. New York, NY: Palgrave.

Gordin, D. N. and Pea, R. D. (1995) "Prospects for Scientific Visualization as an Educational Technology". *Journal of the Learning Sciences*, 4(3):249–79.

Greenberg, R. (1992). "Scanning the Images of Science". *The Science Teacher* (National Science Teachers Association) (0036–8555), 59(8):14.

Greenberg, R., Kolvoord, R.A., Magisos, M., Strom, R.G., and Croft, S. (1993) "Image Processing for Teaching". *Journal of Science Education and Technology*, 1(3): 469–80.

Hagel, H., Brown, S. J., and Davison, L. (2008) "Shaping Strategy in a World of Constant Disruption". *Harvard Business Review* 86(10):80–89.

Henriques, L. (2002) "Children's Ideas about Weather: A Review of the Literature". *School Science and Mathematics* 102(5): 202–15.

Huizinga, J. (1955) *Homo Ludens: A Study of the Play-Element in Culture*. Boston: Beacon Press.

Hung, D., Lee, S.-S., and Lim K.Y.T. (2012) "Authenticity in Learning for the 21st Century: Bridging the Formal and the Informal". *Educational Technology Research & Development*, 60(6):1071–91.

Koker, T., & Rowe, B. (1993). *ChemViz: An NSF-Sponsored Program to Bring High Performance Computing to America's High Schools*. [Machine Readable Data File]. Urbana-Champaign: University of Illinois, National Center for Supercomputing Applications ChemViz Project (Producer). Urbana-Champaign: University of Illinois, National Center for Supercomputing Applications (Distributor).

Kong, L. (2000) "Nature's Dangers, Nature's Pleasures: Urban Children and the Natural World". In S. Holloway and G. Valentine (eds.). *Children's Geographies: Living, Playing, Learning*. London: Routledge.

Kong, L., Yuen, B., Sodhi, N. and Briffett, C. (1999) "The Construction and Experience of Nature: Perspectives of Urban Youths". *Tijdschrift voor Economische en Sociale Geografie*. 90(1): 3–16.

Ku, C.-H., Ho, Y.C., Peng, J.-Y., and Tsai, Y.J. (2012) "Pictorial Metaphors in Typhoon Forecast Charts: An Analysis Based on the Theories of Conceptual Metaphor and Conceptual Blending". Paper presented at the *Annual Conference of the American Society for Engineering Education*, San Antonio TX.

Lim, K.Y.T. (ed.). (2015) *Disciplinary Intuitions and the Design of Learning Environments*. Dordrecht, The Netherlands: Springer.

Narayan, K.M., Gregg, E.W., Engelau, M.M., Moore, B. et al. (2000) "Translation Research for Chronic Disease: The Case of Diabetes". *Diabetes Care* 23:1794–98.

Polito, E., Tanner, K.D., and Monteverdi, J.P. (2008) *Assessing Middle School and College Students' Conceptions About Tornadoes and Other Weather Phenomena*. Proceedings of the *24th Conference on Severe Local Storms*. Savannah, Georgia. http://tornado.sfsu.edu/Activities/SLS_Conference_2008/PolitoDocs/extendab_ejp.pdf [05-18-2010]

Rappaport, E.D. (2009) "What Undergraduates Think About Clouds and Fog". Journal of Geoscience Education 57(2):145–51. doi: http://dx.doi.org/10.5408/1.3544249.

Singer, J., Marx, R.W., and Krajcik, J. (2000) "Constructing Extended Inquiry Projects: Curriculum
Materials for Science Education Reform". *Educational Psychologist*, 35(3): 165–78.
Sweller, J. (1988) "Cognitive Load During Problem Solving: Effects on Learning". *Cognitive Science* 12: 257–85.
Tan, K.C.D., Hedberg, J.G., Koh, T.S., and Seah, W.C. (2006) "Datalogging in Singapore Schools: Supporting Effective Implementations". *Research in Science & Technological Education* 24(1):111–27.

CHAPTER SIX

FABLEARN, FABLAB, MAKERED, EXPERIMENTAL LABORATORIES: TOWARDS A DISCUSSION OF A THEORY OF MAKER EDUCATION FROM A BRAZILIAN PERSPECTIVE

RODRIGO BARBOSA E SILVA
AND LUIZ ERNESTO MERKLE

Introduction

In the final chapter of this book, we will discuss ideas behind maker projects and action in Brazil. Our reflections are not limited to a Brazilian context. As we discuss worldwide concepts, such as FabLab, Maker Education, FabLearn, different "maker movements" around the world can promote a native approximation between their educational literature and thoughts with maker practices in each region or country. It tends to an epistemological background based on progressive education, and science, technology and society – STS – studies in order to support pedagogically the concept of meaningful making. It means that we are promoting a discussion that is not neutral: it has the objective of exploring making in the sense of critical and engaged education with digital technologies and towards freedom; that is why it is based largely around native Brazilian authors. We do not deny that traditional – and, in our case, international – authors such as Papert and Resnick have contributed to the understanding of digital making in Brazilian education; their work is frequently appropriated by Brazilian researchers and groups. These authors and their ideas are important when discussing digital technologies in education but we postulate that our Brazilian experiences have enough contradictions to support ideas in a place identified as a "developing country".

We are pursuing this objective through the philosophy of technology, especially based on Álvaro Vieira Pinto; on Paulo Freire's thoughts and ideas, as Paulo Blikstein has already done in his research; and on FabLearn, a Blikstein proposal that is largely based on Paulo Freire's proposals. We recognise that FabLearn is an effort based at Stanford University, a fact that constitutes firstly a clear example that we agree that Brazil is an international and intellectual giant; secondly, that Paulo Freire is even more referenced, applied and studied abroad than in our Brazilian academia; and thirdly, that the worldwide network FabLearn has found its roots in a Brazilian slum (Blikstein 2008). In this chapter, we first explore ideas behind making in education in four main concepts: traditional FabLab (Gershenfeld 2012), Maker Education (Deloitte and Maker Media 2014), FabLearn (Blikstein 2013) and Experimental Laboratories (*Laboratórios Experimentais*); this last as a critic of the "Californian utopia" (Evangelista 2011). These four concepts offer important elements to fill the theoretical gap presented by the maker movement. Theoretical gaps privilege the misunderstanding that technology constitutes an end in itself, a fact that justifies the importance of a theoretical discussion about digital construction in schools. Under-theorisation of the maker movement was also identified by Worsley and Blikstein (2016).

> We believe that not only is the "maker movement" under theorized (Gomez 2012) but it's (sp.) very under-theorization and anti-intellectualism (often dressed as a rebellious "enfant terrible" against traditional schooling) are part of its culture, which constitute a vicious circle that has engulfed promising education innovation in the past – frenetically implementing new technologies in schools as if their efficacy was self-evident, without carefully demonstrating it.

In this chapter we give special attention to Álvaro Vieira Pinto. Our research group is promoting an effort materialised in several works, e.g., (Barbosa e Silva 2012, Queluz and Merkle 2012 and Gonzatto 2014), discussing and rediscovering Vieira Pinto's work within Brazilian academia. Vieira Pinto presents philosophical resources with which to understand Brazilian questions and projects putting technology in the hands of people. His work gives us a glimpse into the idea that projects, action and ideas are based on people's intrinsically human and interesting work. These efforts around Vieira Pinto's work could support digital fabrication projects and actions designed to understand meaningful making through Paulo Freire's lens, thus we postulate that Vieira Pinto offers a philosophical and nationalist basis for those interested in a Freirean approach to the maker movement. As Vieira Pinto stated, the theory of knowledge is based on the practice of knowledge, thus we bring to this chapter experience with robotics education in order to support our assumptions and postulates regarding digital making in education. These experiences within the public education context give us practical bases from which to propose epistemological and engaged support for making in Brazilian education. Thus, we begin with a description of different concepts of digital fabrication laboratories. We then present a practical experience in robotics education in public schools in Brazil. We conclude with Vieira Pinto's thoughts and critics mainly of the "new industrial revolution" and other emergent issues about technologies.

Concepts of fabrication laboratories

The maker movement has become a matter of growing interest for educators, public authorities and academic researchers in Brazil. This discussion is mainly based on a supposition that technology itself has the power to change our school system. This misleading comprehension, plus the natural enchantment of technologies, led the public sector in Brazil to adopt educational projects before they had been critically reviewed and academically researched; therefore technologies are used in a sense of "eternal solution" (Anderson 2012,2). According to Blikstein,

> Technology embodies the connotation of sudden and irresistible change, with apparently very little effort – a perfect combination. In 1922, Thomas Edison opined that motion pictures would soon replace textbooks, allowing the educational system to run at "100 percent efficiency." This was in the same era of progressive reform that saw the widespread adoption of radio, "the textbooks of the air," and, later, educational television. Since then, the cycles of innovation in educational technology have turned ever more rapidly to include computer labs, laptops, interactive whiteboards, internet, online video, personalized tutors, mobile phones, and tablets. (2014, 2)

Digital technologies are often intended to improve performance (Blikstein 2014), but the question should be how to promote equity and diversity through technologies and people, projects and powerful idea according to the theme proposed by FabLearn during the Brazil 2016 conference. Both Blikstein's concerns about technology as an eternal solution and FabLearn's challenge towards equity and diversity can be fulfilled by principles, such as motivation and epistemological approach, of historical research and practices with technologies in education. These principles and practices, as technologies themselves, are not neutral (Dagnino 2006), just as education is not neutral (Freire 1996, 11). The fact is that establishing a theory that will lead our schooling system to a practice is an act of power; as Carnoy stated, "… the quantity and the nature of schooling process can be and is used to maintain the hierarchical roles of different groups in the society from one generation to the next" (Carnoy 1974, 15).

In the next four subsections, we discuss distinct concepts of digital fabrication that base action and projects within the Brazilian educational and social context. These concepts underlie projects of digital construction in Brazil, thus exposing their similarities, perspectives and contradictions, which will contribute to a more critical adoption of these practices in education. It is important to understand the differences between proposals such as FabLab, more suitable to civil and commercial actions, and Fab Learn, which discusses and expands educational research on technologies and education.

The traditional FabLab concept

The acronym "FabLab" identifies shared spaces dedicated to prototyping and digital fabrication organised under an international network of shared knowledge, practices and, as we argue in this chapter, common ideas of how the "FabLab movement" is or should be shaped and adopted around the world. Even in a Brazilian context, the label "FabLab" was adopted to identify digital construction spaces such as *FabLab Livre* (Free FabLab), São Paulo (Inst. de Tecnologia Social 2016), an initiative promoted by the local government of the city of São Paulo; and Insper FabLab (INSPER 2016), a space dedicated to engineering courses in a private college in São Paulo. Indeed, according to the Ministry of Science, Technology and Innovation in Brazil (Min. do Desenvolvimento Industria e Comercio Exterior 2014, 128), a group of spaces such as *Laboratório de Design, Inovação e Sustentabilidade* (LABDIS/UFRJ*); Laboratório de Design e Seleção de Materiais* (LDSM/UFRGS); FABLAB Brasil; Instituto Nacional de Tecnologia, and many other places and services maintained by *Serviço Nacional da Indústria* (SENAI) are bonded to the idea of design laboratories in the same sense of a FabLab. The term "FabLab" does not offer a direct translation in Portuguese, thus it is adopted in its original English by those institutions providing a design space. Widely recognised as the father of FabLabs, Gershenfeld (Barbosa e Silva and Merkle 2016, 47) explains the central idea behind these spaces: initially "FabLab" was conceived to identify "fabrication labs" or "fabulous labs". Nowadays, the lab described by Gershenfeld's work is a global network, started in the Center of Bits and Atoms of the Massachusetts Institute of

Technology in 2003. It is not only a fabrication laboratory, indeed it is not a fabulous laboratory, but it is surely a world class network of spaces and people offering support to an idea. The FabLab idea continues to spread around the world with the support of the Fab Foundation, a US non-profit organisation (Fab Foundation 2016). All FabLabs preserve core capabilities, according to Gershenfeld: as "part of a larger 'maker movement' of high-tech 'do-it-yourselfs'", the FabLab is understood as a space to democratic access to technological tools, and to design and share files to local production based in equipment like 3D printers (Gershenfeld 2012, 48). Gershenfeld (ibid) states that FabLabs will have "revolutionary implications for industry" and it constitutes a "new industrial revolution".

> The first Industrial Revolution can be traced back to 1761, when the Bridgewater Canal opened in Manchester, England. Commissioned by the Duke of Bridgewater to bring coal from his mines in Worsley to Manchester and to ship products made with that coal out to the world, it was the first canal that did not follow an existing waterway. [...] Now, Manchester has an innovative fab lab that is taking part in a new industrial revolution. A design created there can be sent electronically anywhere in the world for on-demand production, which effectively eliminates the cost of shipping. And unlike the old mills, the means of production can be owned by anyone.

Although preserving "core capabilities" is not a limitation, a FabLab can be understood as the pillar of a broad maker movement that cultivates the equalisation and worldwide replication of practices tested inside the network. The FabLab network is an advantage when starting a makerspace, but it represents almost a regulation of a model of fabrication laboratory. It represents the materialisation of an idea of new industrial revolution, indeed. It is fair to recognise that the roots of the FabLab are grounded in an educational perspective on MIT, but its history follows a path of commercial and civil organisations. As an educational approach to technologies, FabLab does not present important elements to formal educational environments, especially to elementary and middle schools. In the same sense, the next section highlights the Maker Faire concept, maybe the most publicised action towards digital construction. As with FabLab concepts, Maker Faire® is an object of interest and discussions in the educational arena.

"Maker Faire" concept

Maker Faire is a worldwide network of events making a huge impact in the so-called maker movement. It is also a trademark owned by Maker

Media Inc. Its actions are based on enthusiasts, hobbyists, professionals, and an uncountable number of followers around the world. The first author of this chapter has experience as a speaker in two Maker Faires: Rome 2014 and the Bay Area 2016. In sum, Maker Faire has its own educational arm, called MakerEd. Although they appear to be and are presented as two independent organisations – probably they are independent, at least officially – the objectives, aims, practices and ideas behind Maker Ed are strongly attached to those propagated by Maker Inc. It is fair to say that Maker Inc., Faire, Make Magazine and books issued by authors such as Chris Anderson (2012) constitute the "royalty" of a Maker public vision nowadays. It is largely understandable if we consider that Maker Media owns Make Magazine and Maker Faire trademarks, and that ownership jump-started the "publisher's" (Blikstein 2014) maker movement. As we recognise that Maker Media has succeeded in promoting several Maker Faires, it is time to ask if this publisher's maker movement is suitable in schools.

We observe that the Maker Media concept is strongly linked to the idea of a "new industrial revolution", as Anderson stated in his book *Makers: The New Industrial Revolution* (2012). It frequently presents the ideas of a new age, new concepts and new forms of doing things: as Maker Media proclaims, "The launch of Make: magazine in 2005, followed by Maker Faire in 2006, jump-started a worldwide maker movement, *which is transforming innovation, culture and education*" (Maker Media 2016, authors' emphasis). It sounds out the traditional discourse of transforming society, culture and education through technologies or technological practices. This kind of idea ignores the idea that humans, in society, are the main actors promoting changes and transformations. In real educational systems, these ideas do not match concepts such as equity, diversity and freedom, mainly due to the conceptual background of ideas from Anderson and Maker Media. As inspiration, Anderson quotes the work of Friedrich Hayek, a liberal economist, in order to discuss why centralised organisations exist. Anderson (2012, 144) quotes a concept derived from Hayek's work.

> In his own landmark paper in 1945, "The Use of Information in Society", Hayek observed that knowledge is unevenly distributed among people and that centralized planned and coordinated organizations would be unable to tap distributed knowledge (his point: only free markets could).

According to Anderson (2012, 145), the answer to this challenge is communities.

> Communities tend to be more egalitarian, in part because they typically don't have the same legal obligations and risk as a company. They don't have to check references and get people to sign contracts before they participate, the way a company typically must. They can afford to take more chances with participants, because the consequences of things not working out are so much smaller when you're not promising people a wage (not to say they can't get paid for work done, but any rewards tend to come after the fact, not as a salary).

Assuming Hayek's (1983) argument that centralised organisations are unable to "tap distributed knowledge", the ideas behind Anderson denote a fundamental contradiction of the FabLab and Maker Faire concepts. The maker movement can be assumed as several groups of "communities" doing things but their ideas are centralised in efforts such as FabLab (MIT) and Maker Inc. Indeed, the very concept of the existence of organisations "unable" to tap distributed knowledge demonstrates the central point of the reception of Hayek's ideas in education; namely, the idea that education is not a social effort but an individual endeavour. Hayek argues that the government should not manage schools, and society shall privilege the most capable in each group (1983, 483). These kinds of ideas give the necessary support to the liberal notion of sorting people to identify the most capable; the education system accomplishes this most efficiently. The idea of the self-made man is also present within the concept of "Maker" in the sense of an *enfant terrible* or hacker, meaning a solitary problem solver. Other elements that allow us to understand that such a liberal concept is not suitable for education come from a summit promoted by Maker Media and the Deloitte Consulting Company. After discussion, they released a report stating that the maker movement will have a "disruptive impact on traditional educational institutions as it shifts the practice and sets the stage for more distributed and sustained active learning where the individual seeks out and crafts educational experiences" (Deloitte and Maker Media 2014). Furthermore, the concept of "student" in this report is frequently confused with the concept of "workforce", denoting that it is based on the idea of a world where societal factors are not really taken into account.

These three ideas – firstly, "transforming innovation, culture and education"; secondly, the critics of "centralised organisations" and the proposal of a community as a "more egalitarian" model; and thirdly, the "disruptive impact on traditional educational institutions" – help us understand that the Maker Faire concept incorporates the ideas of the self-made man, the new industrial revolution, and education as a private and individual effort. This kind of ideological support is important to understanding the public assumption of the maker as an *enfant terrible*, a hacker (Blikstein and Worsley 2016), but it is far from the equity demanded by public educational institutions. In contrast, we present in the next two sections proposals linked more with the idea of education as a public and social effort.

Experimental laboratories

Experimental laboratories, or *Laboratórios Experimentais* in Portuguese, is a term proposed by Fonseca to identify several design spaces such as "media labs, hackerspaces, FabLabs" (Fab Foundation 2016), which denotes that Fonseca is highlighting the experimental characteristics of these spaces. Fonseca's thesis was advised by Evangelista, a professor at the University of Campinas. Evangelista critiques the "Californian ideology" (Evangelista 2011; Fonseca 2014).

> This set of ideas, practices and techno-productive mobilizations would be only an eccentricity if it was not an overlap with a form of thinking and of viewing of the world with high influence power since the 1990's at least. It was named by Richard Barbrook and Andy Cameron as the "Californian ideology".

Evangelista's criticisms of the Californian ideology help us to understand concepts published mainly by Maker Media: Maker Faire-like initiatives base their ideas on vision of the world from Silicon Valley experiences, ideas, practices and interests. Silicon Valley's vision of the world is identified in ideas from Maker Media and Deloitte as education to "prepare the workforce". As an alternative to this utilitarian view of the world, Fonseca promoted a study in Brazil in 2014, sponsored by the Brazilian Ministry of Culture (Ministério da Cultura do Brasil). The first fact to note is that Experimental Labs, in this case, are under the culture public sector, not under the Brazilian educational authority, MEC (Ministry of Education, or Ministério da Educação). This constitutes a major fact as, in recent Brazilian history, the Ministry of Culture promoted actions towards "free knowledge", materialised in public policy based on Creative Commons licensing, free software and open hardware. Fonseca struggles against the idea of "all" experimental laboratories being descendants of the MIT initiatives (Fonseca 2014), such as FabLab spin-offs. He states that

> The idea of a decentralized network of independent spaces, where not only internet access but objects fabrication indeed, among other implications in

> order to decrease the tributary control upon goods circulation, fits techno utopian aspirations. It is not a coincidence that one of heavyweight names, Chris Anderson, former editor of Wired Magazine and coordinator of TED, affirms maker culture as a platform to the new industrial revolution.

It is important to understand that there is no neutral technology to be passively adopted – proposals coming from Silicon Valley towards the world need to be analysed first. It is a fact that the majority of computational tools used nowadays are based on Silicon Valley or Bay Area innovations. But in reality, this Californian ideology is in large part based on assumptions outside the Bay Area. Nonetheless, this ideology is more accepted by its admirers than its practitioners. It is true that there is a message from California-located people, such as Anderson, that the world is entering a new industrial revolution, but this message can also be found in other discourses, including in Brazil. The critics of the Californian utopia can be understood by science, technology and society studies as a critic of the technological determinism broadly presented in projects and actions using computers in public education in Brazil.

In fact, experimental laboratories propose that design spaces should be an alternative to commercial laboratories. Fonseca argues that, in the USA, MIT's Media Lab is "almost completely incorporated by the industry" (2014, 44). It happened, according to Fonseca, after an appropriation, by the US industry, of the counterculture movement that flourished in the US in the 1960–70s. These experimental laboratories were established under the Ministry of Culture in Brazil during the last decade under a network called RedeLabs (Fonseca 2014): Experimental Arrangements of Creative Culture (*Arranjos Experimentais de Cultura Criativa*) identified Brazilian initiatives in this area, such as *Nuvem – estação rural de arte e tecnologia* from Rio de Janeiro; Vivolab, Artemov, Circuito Artmov, Networked Hacklab and Labmovel from São Paulo; and other spaces in Belém and Santarém, Pará, Cachoeira e Salvador, Bahia; Visconde de Mauá, Rio de Janeiro; and Belo Horizonte, Minas Gerais (Fonseca and Fleischman 2014). This research on experimental laboratories identifies that Brazil has promoted such spaces in authentic ways, even when based on fiscal renounces and/or private support (the "S" system in Brazil is a variety of official entities maintained by the private sector but sponsored by public taxes, with contributions mainly through workers' earnings).

As for the critics of the Californian ideology, it is fair to recognise that not every initiative from California embodies this "ideology". Just as we cannot assume that there is only one carioca or paulista culture, we cannot assume that there is only one Californian culture; nonetheless, the critique to the liberal approach from Maker Media is valuable to understanding the interests and bias of the published maker movement. In the next section, we briefly comment on a Brazilian / Californian initiative that is more Freire than Hayek: namely, FabLearn.

FabLearn

FabLabs, Makerspaces, Hackerspaces and others share the idea of a social, communitarian or commercial space. It could be shared with partners, enthusiasts, fellows or clients, and its access is, in short, free for interested or invited people. But school is not really a space only for interested or invited people because education is assumed to be a social need, and an individual journey to a profession or a position in the social structure. From an individual perspective, education is a unique way to become more prepared for the challenges of a social and professional life; from a social perspective, education is the guarantee that society will have a continuum, and be organised as a system. Regarding fabrication laboratories in schools, they present the fundamental characteristic of being used by a diverse audience, a more accurate social portrait of each society. We recognise that education, as a system, tends to create barriers and exclude people; with these learning spaces, a vast number of different persons, perspectives and cultures will have access to fabrication tools.

A special characteristic about FabLearn justifies Brazilian interest in a proposal by Stanford University: Paulo Blikstein, principal at the Transformative Learning Technologies Lab – TTL – is a Brazilian-born educator. Also, FabLearn is based on progressive education, especially on Papert's works towards democratising computers among students. Blikstein (2015, xv) argues, "You cannot think about thinking without thinking about what Seymour Papert would think. There is a paradox in education: the closer the world comes to realising Seymour Papert's vision, the less his work is remembered". Indeed, FabLearn is deeply inspired by Paulo Freire, the patron of Brazilian education. This inspiration is notably present in several texts issued by Blikstein, such as *Travels in Troy with Freire* (2008) and "Digital Fabrication and 'Making' in Education: The Democratization of Invention" (2013). We advocate a Freirean approach to digital construction efforts in Brazil: we need strong theoretical pillars to understand how school historically deals with technologies and pedagogical questions, and to base projects on *lato sensu* ideas such as diversity and equity in making. Of course there is no technological tool promoting by itself diversity and equity; however, there are meaningful ideas derived from those authors that support human actions towards diversity and equity. These ideas and values support decisions such as promoting a making space and giving attention to concepts such as "new industrial revolution" or "meaningful making".

Making in education is not new. We can identify dozens of research projects, academic studies and even commercial products that have been used for decades. Logo, Lego, Gogo Board and hundreds of technological platforms can be easily found in past works on technology and education. That is why it is important to verify what has happened in order to better understand the future of digital fabrication in education. Blikstein (2013, 1–3) identifies historic attempts to bring computers and electronic technologies to schools, and describes the early years of computers at schools, arguing about "the democratisation of invention": "Computers in those years were large, expensive, awkward machines, and the idea of using them as a medium for personal expression and learning was inconceivable". Notwithstanding, according to Blikstein, researchers like Papert, Resnick and Wilensky were hard at work to make the use of computers at school possible. The most recognisable technological resource that appeared from this work, known worldwide, is the Logo language, thus

> the world caught up with the idea that not only could computational media be a vehicle for powerful ideas in mathematics, engineering, and science – an important new kind of literacy – but it was an approachable activity in schools. (Blikstein 2013, 2)

Blikstein argues that digital fabrication is a new field with which to explore informatics and computers in education; in short, it fulfils Papert's vision of the computer as the "Children's Machine" (Papert 2008). Moreover, the new approach of digital construction is a new chance as computers in schools could comprehend diverse knowledge and practices such as arts, design and engineering:

> The analogy with the development of Logo is clear: simultaneously, digital fabrication technology became better and more accessible, and the intellectual activities enabled by the new technology became more valued and important. What Logo did for geometry and programming – bringing complex mathematics within the reach of schoolchildren – fabrication labs can do for design and engineering. Digital fabrication is Logo for atoms. (Blikstein 2008, 2)

Blikstein alerts us to a special concern about computing at school, the "experts" problem: "Every few decades or centuries, a new set of skills and intellectual activities become crucial for work, conviviality, and citizenship – often democratizing tasks and skills previously only accessible to experts" (6). The key point is that a new set of technologies is, more often, seen as a tool for experts. Apart from the price, conditions, development and "democratisation", a key point emerges: how a specific society of users absorbs this new wave. Our intent in this chapter is to discuss a maker education theory based on Brazilian experiences, and we discuss these experiences based on Brazilian authors, theories and ideas. The next section will bring the highlights of an experience on robotics education in Brazil. It is followed by a theoretical discussion based on Vieira Pinto's thoughts.

Practice supporting theory

This section presents a practice based on robotics education and free software in order to base theories on the maker movement in Brazil. Our assumptions are largely based on the idea of education as a social and collective effort. We argue that technological education is not only a deterministic way towards better workforce training but also an effort that elevates our society as a public benefit. The case that we bring to this essay is a robotics education action that occurred between 2009 and 2012 in a city in Brazil's south; it was led by the first author of this chapter and by engineer Luiz Rodrigo Grochocki. It brought robotics education to a group of public schools and involved nearly 40 educators with different backgrounds in formal education: there were educators with a background/major in fields such as history, pedagogy, technical drawing and maths, among others. The experience was based on the SuperLogo programming language, the Brazilian version of Logo provided by Unicamp (Nucleo de Informatica Aplicada a Educacao 2000), and Gogo Board (Sipitakiat, Blikstein and Cavallo 2004), an open hardware platform for robotics education. The term "maker" was not famous at that time in Brazil; nevertheless, students used raw materials from electronic garbage in order to classify, collect and reuse sensors, motors, wires and other previously discarded materials. Prior to robotics education, computer laboratories were, in the majority, traditional, i.e., computers disposed in a line, or were non-existent or unstructured. The most visible effect of this persistent traditional use of computers in education is that public schools are using computers as a blackboard metaphor; due to constraints in space and time, meaningful activities with technology are rarely practised. Robotics education, as well the maker movement nowadays, can be considered a "political subversive agenda" (Blikstein 2008) planted inside teachers' and students' minds. However, a subversive political agenda does not come without contradictions and struggles against it. Such contradictions and struggles are the same that any proposal for innovative work with technologies will suffer when it goes to schools. Next, we will show successful cases of this initiative and then we will focus on the challenges.

Rural schools

Our experience with several schools showed us that rural institutions performed better in terms of dedication and interest. It was completely unexpected by local educational authorities that a distant school could be the most prominent example of success. Some students did not have access to electricity in their houses, nor did they have electronic toys or computers. This lack of access to electronics is the best explanation of why they dedicated themselves to robotics activities; indeed, they expanded it to an unplanned after-school programme. The rural school dedicated the time to construct meaningful devices linked to their own experiences. For instance, they made brooders, incubators, an irrigation system, and grain milling systems. According to the reports issued by the teacher in charge, after an initial resistance, the children become very interested in how technologies could solve their problems. They promoted regular fairs in order to show parents, the community and their peers their robots and computer programs.

Restructuring laboratories

Making activities such as robotics education have the power to change the established routine in traditional computer laboratories. Government programmes bring computers to schools but in a traditional layout: computers disposed as row upon row of desktop computers. These computers were used for traditional activities such as internet access and gaming. Robotics brought to these traditional computer labs new tools, such as screwdrivers, pliers, wire, batteries and electronic scrap. These new elements made the labs more chaotic but also more attractive to children. Also, Logo programming language was an element that attracted a lot of attention as controlling the computer was new to these children. The lesson from this topic is that new elements give children the chance to experience new activities, new ideas and new forms of learning. Indeed, this potential is present in makerspaces that provide tools, practices and approach not usual to traditional constrcuts of education.

Non-curricular experiences

Curricula constitute a major concern in Brazilian schools. Teachers are trained to apply a curriculum, children are trained to absorb and "know" curricula, and parents expect that the content be "well done" by the educational system. Although this system is well accepted, technologies bring the idea of change, thus it is a chance for progressive educators to promote new forms of learning. Subjects such as labour conditions, local problems, the transportation system and other issues related to daily life worked as themes for robotics. The absence of a classificatory evaluation system can also be highlighted as positive: it allowed free experimentation and no worries about grades. The main objective was the open fair, which each school promoted in order to promote their creations.

Lack of support from the pedagogical team

At the same time technology brings the idea of the "new", it also carries an image of being complicated, not accessible, and impossible for disadvantaged schools. A pedagogical team is a centralised group of educators in charge of planning in public education systems. They expect to control educational projects with schedules, step-by-step lessons and no contradictions. In short, the disciplinary system is embodied by the school's administration. This is particularly trouble for open technological proposals in which the protagonist shifts from the planned to discovery, and from the teacher (and the system itself) as a provider to the teacher as a guide. Such thought is based on an assumption that every single detail of every single activity in a school must be described in worksheets and workbooks, and measured in structured assessments. Although we can identify a growing discourse akin to exploratory technologies in schools, school culture is strong in the term Papert identified decades ago – the immunological reaction of school (Papert 1997, 2008).

Competition with other projects

Schools are the natural place for every kind of project. Ethics, sports, drugs prevention, sexual education, religion, civic duties and entrepreneurship are among the dozens of topics covered in regular or extra-class activities. Obviously, all topics are important but a school has to prioritise some of them. From the second year of the robotics education initiative, another project was vying for the space in the computer labs: entrepreneurial pedagogy (*Pedagogia Empreendedora*). At a time when entrepreneurship is more commented on than stimulated by public efforts, it sounded like a good idea to "prepare" children for an "entrepreneurial world". This kind of project is normally more structured in terms of traditional schooling – with workbooks, some competition and deadlines. The contrast with an open initiative such as robotics is remarkable: ironically, robotics requires more hard work and free exploration than those types of project. Notwithstanding the intrinsic "entrepreneurial" characteristics of a maker initiative, robotics education, digital construction and even programming are activities that demand convincing the pedagogical team about that fact.

Lame duck syndrome

"Lame duck" is a term that describes an elected authority whose successor has been elected. In Brazil, it means that the government's projects will end when the new authority takes office. This was the case in the robotics education initiative: when the opposition won the elections, all projects were delayed or ended. This is particularly problematic because such initiatives need time to be completely understood and appropriated by teachers and the school community. If one is considering large-scale maker initiatives in the public sector, one must be conscious that political changes matter even in terms of pedagogical and logistical support.

A theory supporting making

In the preceding sections, we described four concepts of digital fabrication and the highlights from a practical experience in public schools in Brazil. Both proposals and practices are important to understand and reinforce diversity and equity in making at schools. As there are no neutral technologies, we assume that there are no neutral concepts or practice. If one is considering a makerspace in education, choosing between a FabLab model or a FabLearn model has implications on the practices, perspectives and learning path of students and educators. It is a social issue because the choice of a technological model is a choice of a model of education. Each option has its own potentials and limitations but some of them are less suitable for education, just as some are less adherent to commercial or industrial uses. In order to aid the better understanding of making as an educational resource, we offer in the next section thoughts extracted from Álvaro Vieira Pinto.

Álvaro Vieira Pinto

Álvaro Borges Vieira Pinto was a philosopher with expressive work during the 1950–70s in Brazilian history. This period hosted internal discussions about national developmentalism; one of the arenas of this discussion – the Superior Institute of Brazilian Studies (*Instituto Superior de Estudos Brasileiros* in Portuguese) – was led by Álvaro Vieira Pinto. This government institute was established after the Getúlio Vargas presidential term, and it was closed at the beginning of the military *coup d'état* in 1964. In Brazil, that period is identified with the ideal of "national developmentalism"; i.e., discussions about industrialisation at the elite level and the insertion of excluded people in the economic and social process at a progressive level. Although the term "national development" was a subject of major importance in Brazil at that time, there were discussions about the tendency of that development: on the one hand, the "national developmentalism" bias was more attached to the interests of the national elite and to a compromise of not opposing the national development of the balance of power during that time. On the other hand, another ideal was inclined to a disruption between social classes: "economic nationalism". Queluz and Merkle (2012) argue that Vieira Pinto's thoughts are consistent with economic nationalism, thus we can understand Vieira Pinto as interested in national development based on a rupture in the ruling social and economic system. In practice, it meant reforms in laws about land property and the workers' rights, and furthermore the opening of Brazil to the international market. Queluz and Merkle's study tests whether Vieira Pinto's works were based on the ideas of an "expansion of citizen's rights" and combating oligarchic interests.

In 1964, after President João Goulart's deposition by a civil-military *coup d'état*, hundreds of intellectuals, professors and political activists were exiled from Brazilian territory, including Álvaro Vieira Pinto. After his return to Brazil in 1968, Vieira Pinto stayed in Rio de Janeiro to work on unpublished manuscripts. One of those was the *Concept of Technology*, a work finished in 1973 and released to the public only in 2008. The military dictatorship in Brazil lasted from 1964 to 1985, a period when Vieira Pinto, Paulo Freire and an uncountable number of thinkers were excluded from Brazilian public life. "Subversive" thinkers were accused of being "enemies of the regime"; thus exile abroad was the only option for most of them. Vieira Pinto's books have only recently been recovered and now Brazilian academia finally has the opportunity to discuss one of its most prominent national philosophers. Vieira Pinto dedicated his thoughts to understanding national development from an emancipatory approach, and his most powerful work is a two-volume book called *The Concept of Technology* (2005) (*O Conceito de Tecnologia*). Vieira Pinto's thoughts on national development in a non-conventional way (or, at least, in a way distant from the interests of the national elites) are remarkable in his work about technology (2005) and education (2005). What Vieira Pinto tells us is that we, as a developing nation, must deal with questions such as empowering, recognise our population and produce our own solutions to our problems. By doing this, we can reinforce our society's goals in order to support a better education system.

Vieira Pinto, techniques and technologies

Vieira Pinto points to a social effort that will help people in the "developing world" deal with solutions to their societal needs in their own way with. The word used at the time to identify the emerging electronic technologies was "cybernetic", which can be considered a label for a human endeavour that society uses to sustain itself with technologies and techniques such as informatics and programming, among others, in the sense of human expansion. Cybernetics is an expanded understanding of the current computing technologies as a component registered and subscribed to living beings and confined to human needs and projects. It also denotes a historical accumulation of the understanding of techniques and technologies evolving from contradictions of societies in relationship to the world. Technology, understood from the perspective of Vieira Pinto, is a human expansion that leads us to think that we do not live in an era of unprecedented technological grandeur but in an age in which mankind is placed as a producer of technical and technological artefacts to meet the demands of future projects. This is different from thinking of the resumption of history, or the "new industrial revolution", a term in vogue in maker debates less concerned with the understanding of social relations through technologies. Also for Vieira Pinto, technology can aid the interpretation of the limited reality of a society rather than a reinforcement tool of dependence and domination. Thus, cybernetics represents a "serious and useful knowledge" (Vieira Pinto 2005, 657–59).

Through the lens of Vieira Pinto, technologies inspire the exploration of the maker movement in the sense of creating our own pedagogical proposals, practices and models, not strictly linked to external discussions, as in Maker Faire. Those "externalist" discussions are usually disconnected from Brazilian contradictions, mainly because they lack a critical review which could lead to welcoming them as neutral, ignoring national educational issues. The intention of our theoretical discussion is to support the proposed ideas and local contradictions. By doing this, Brazil will value practices of experiences in technological education constituted historically. As an example of Brazilian initiatives that value local aspects and historical, there is the Innovation Lab in Education, *Univali Itajaí*, that, in addition to traditional electro-electronic technologies, provides an opportunity to practice woodwork in a digital makerspace (Raabe 2015).

As the maker movement in schools requires national theoretical contributions, Vieira Pinto shows that it is necessary to expand the knowledge and effort needed to develop technologies that will lead to understanding the national reality. Simple repetition is not enough to further the understanding of the circumscribed problems. According to Vieira Pinto (2005, 25),

> Only a change in the methodology course, the design and the problem of dialectical analysis of knowledge and interpretation, also dialectics, its algorithmic transposition or heuristics to the data processor devices can lead to a new direction, to secure progress, rich, unique and ascending.

Vieira Pinto's advice, for change in the methodological direction, has the potential to be used as a basis for making activities in Brazilian education. It is not enough to follow internationally accepted waves; it is important to establish a project inspired by computing discussions as proposed by Vieira Pinto, i.e., the heuristic transposition of the instrumental in one direction, that of progress. For the philosopher, cybernetics as a complete solution is an old project based on Descartes and Leibniz: *mathesis universalis*. The question for Vieira Pinto, should the judge become able to instruct himself in the abstract reason, combining physical and logical quantification? It is important to note that there is a discourse that situates the computer and its codes in the maker movement, as in the recent parallel of Vieira Pinto's criticism of the *mathesis universalis* (Vieira Pinto 2005, 647–50). However, each historical period has its own *mathesis universalis*, which was once the train, radio or other technological advances previously considered passports for the future. The material thinking about a technical resource is traditional when it comes to technological advances, as pointed out by Blikstein (2014): Edison believed that the moving images that constitute a film could transform education.

According to Vieira Pinto, there are cybernetic beings made by nature and by creation. The central idea is that "the most perfect computer is only an analog or isomorph of the human brain, because only by construction has the computer possessed qualities, while the living organ is due them to the nature" (2005, 145). Thus, in order to support educational activities, to elaborate digital construction laboratories, students design their own humanity through these activities. They are not projecting "maker things" because they are projecting themselves through it. More importantly, by the feedback provided by these activities, she/he is building himself/herself up for citizenship and work, as well as honing the ability to contribute to the development of society in general.

Discussion and concluding remarks

This chapter debates four concepts of laboratories in order to understand their relationship with an education that contains both diversity and equity. It also presents practical and theoretical aspects of the digital construction applied in public schools. Educators, authorities, school communities and parents considering a maker initiative should observe the progress of other projects in order to know the challenges ahead. Within the educational world, it is very important to base projects, ideas and initiatives in theoretical and practical literature about similar subjects. This is our initial intent: offering theoretical views based on Brazilian philosophy of technology and based on past practices, especially in robotics education, to support a desired future of meaningful making in education.

Among the four concepts exposed throughout this text (FabLab, Maker Faire, Experimental Labs and FabLearn), FabLearn is the most suitable for the context of Brazilian public schools, and it has a practical relationship with the theoretical approach based on Viera Pinto, i.e., an approach that privileges people over technical aspects of technological artefacts. Our last conclusion is based on the acknowledgement that FabLearn presents a Freirean background, and it shows progressive concerns about diversity, equity, freedom and opportunities for students. Indeed, it was conceived based, among other historical facts, on Brazilian experiences (fieldwork in São Paulo) and theories (Paulo Freire), and it is open to an active remix in different situations in Brazil and worldwide. Our assumption is also based on the experiences of robotics education related in a preceding section: those experiences in a public educational system, their success and their challenges, offer a glimpse into our efforts regarding the democratisation of opportunity. Blikstein and Worsley argue that the maker movement is under-theorised, and its under-theorisation is part of its culture. It is time for maker enthusiasts to become more aware of theories and practices. It is a fact that there is not a theory of knowledge, nor a theory of making, but each effort, each new laboratory and each new activity, when discussed and shared with other enthusiasts and with the academia, have the potential to help establish more than one maker theory.

The experiences of educational robotics narrated in this chapter, plus a Brazilian theory of technology based on Vieira Pinto, provide an overview of efforts related to the democratisation of opportunities. Free experiences like these are based on the higher values of a society, but they are constantly being challenged and their evolution is not free of contradictions and disputes. Blikstein and Worsley (2016) have argued that the movement is under-theorised and this sub-theorising is part of the maker culture; thus it is time for enthusiasts and practitioners to become more aware of their practices and the importance of their production to the generation and dissemination of knowledge. There is not only one theory of knowledge, and it is not appropriate to state that there exists or will exist only one maker theory; ongoing efforts in each laboratory, each digital initiative, has the potential to push the necessary maker theories towards consolidation, expansion and democratisation.

Our contribution to this debate is related to science, technology and society studies – STS. We bring this contribution, here based on Álvaro Vieira Pinto, in order to sustain Brazilian thought about technology and education. Vieira Pinto has an extensive philosophical reflection about technology that favours development through democratic inclusion, from the bottom up, thus justifying an approach to free digital construction. This kind of thinking has implications for the daily activities of our society, especially in education. It warns us that digital construction in education can be used to support the empowerment of students and recognise the knowledge of the excluded, as the case of rural school previously mentioned. These activities in a rural school show that there are not only standardised ways of using computers and digital resources in schools; the key point is to provide the freedom in which to practice and try new ideas. This knowledge appears in Vieira Pinto's thoughts on cybernetics: he argues that the goal of technology is be part of the process of human evolution, and technology is used to make the human more human. In schools, this means, firstly, recognising the aspirations and practices of students; secondly, thinking and promoting practical learning by doing; and thirdly, giving value to the relationship between students and their needs as active citizens of society. The perspective is more than mere official recognition because it is the need to provide real labs of digital construction in order to stimulate the freedom to discover new uses and knowledge with technology.

These observations also show challenges beyond the pedagogical, such as the bureaucratic and political aspects of public education. There is much work to be done in order to persuade education authorities about the value of technology in open proposals. Even when delighted with terms like modernity, entrepreneurship, programming and technological era, internal bureaucracy presents initial constraints for projects of this magnitude. The school may be prepared to plan and evaluate every aspect of learning, but learning by doing is not necessarily easy to control and measure. In the Brazilian context, there are problems in the relationship between the teaching staff and the political and institutional spectrum, and these should have the attention of the maker movement in education.

According to Vieira Pinto, cybernetics could represent a dependency or a serious and useful knowledge. Dependency is a traditional theme discussed by actors such as the Free Software Movement. In our case, two open artefacts were adopted: SuperLogo and Gogo Board. This intentionality brings the idea of sharing ideas, projects and knowledge. Although polemic within public education in Brazil, free software and open hardware are good solutions for the contradiction between dependency and useful knowledge, as our practical experience has shown in a preceding section. It means not that only free software and open hardware will provide freedom but also that their practices based on the efforts of communities will offer a path of shared and meaningful practices. That is almost completely forbidden when using closed platforms due to legal and budget restrictions. More than free in a sense of monetary cost, SuperLogo and Gogo Board have brought new practices to teachers and students in relation to the foregoing observations.

Brazilian society demands solutions for the contradictions, theses and ideas presented here. This means an active, critical, continuous and conscientious practice of democracy and freedom with technologies.

Acknowledgement

Our thanks to the Lemann Center for Educational Entrepreneurship and Innovation in Brazil at Stanford for supporting the first author of this chapter as a Visiting Student Researcher at the Graduate School of Education/Stanford from Jan–Jun/2016.

References

Anderson, C. (2012) *Makers: The New Industrial Revolution.* Crown Business, New York, NY, USA.

Barbosa e Silva, R. (2012) *Abordagem crítica de robótica educacional: Álvaro Vieira Pinto e Estudos de Ciência, Tecnologia e Sociedade.* Retrieved March 23, 2014 from http://files.dirppg.ct.utfpr.edu.br/ppgte/dissertacoes/2012/ppgte_dissertacao_371_2012.pdf

Barbosa e Silva, R. and Merkle, L. E. (2016) "Perspectivas educacionais FabLearn: conceitos e práticas maker no Brasil". In *FabLearn Brazil 2016*. Retrieved October 10, 2016 from https://www.academia.edu/28491291/Perspectivas_educacionais_FabLearn_conceitos_e_pr%C3%A1ticas_maker_no_Brasil

Bazzo, W., von Lisingen, I., and Pereira, L.T.V. (2003). *Introdução aos Estudos CTS (Ciência, Tecnologia e Sociedade).* Organização De Estados Ibero-Americanos Para A Educação, A Ciência E A Cultura (OEI), Spain. Retrieved May 20, 2015 from http://www.oei.es/salactsi/Livro_CTS_OEI.pdf

Blikstein, P. (2008) "Travels in Troy with Freire: Technology as an Agent for Emancipation". In P. Noguera and C. A. Torres (eds.), *Social Justice Education for Teachers: Paulo Freire and the Possible Dream.* Sense, Rotterdam, Netherlands, 205–44.

—. (2013) *Digital Fabrication and "Making" in Education: The Democratization of Invention.* In J. Walter-Herrmann and C. Büching (eds.), *FabLabs: Of Machines, Makers and Inventors.* Transcript Publishers, Bielefeld. Retrieved March 19, 2014 from http://www.academia.edu/download/30555959/Blikstein-2013-Making_The_Democratization_of_Invention.pdf.

—. (2014) "Paulo Blikstein, The Maker Movement and Education: The Final Revenge of Progressive Education, or Just Another Fad?" Retrieved July 25, 2014 from http://mondaytalk-berkeley.blogspot.com.br/2014/01/feb-3-paulo-blikstein-maker-movement.html

—. (2014) "Re-empowering Powerful Ideas: Designers' Mission in the Age of Ubiquitous Technology". In *Interaction, Design and Children.* https://doi.org/2593968.2597649.

—. (2015) "Foreword". In Paulo Blikstein, Sylvia Libow Martinez and Heather Allen Pang (eds.), *Meaningful Making: Projects and Inspirations for Fab Labs + Makerspace.* Constructing Modern Knowledge Press, Torrance, CA USA, 158. Retrieved from http://fablearn.stanford.edu/fellows/sites/default/files/Blikstein_Martinez_Pang-Meaningful_Making_book.pdf

Blikstein, P. and Worsley, M. (2016) (forthcoming) "Children are not Hackers: Building a Culture of Powerful Ideas, Deep Learning, and Equity in the Maker Movement". In *Makeology.*

Carnoy, M. (1974) *Education as Cultural Imperialism.* David McKay Company, Inc., New York.

Dagnino, R. (2002) Enfoques sobre a relação Ciência, Tecnologia e Sociedade: Neutralidade e Determinismo. *DataGramaZero – Revista de Ciência da Informação 3*. Retrieved May 15, 2016 from http://www.oei.es/salactsi/rdagnino3.htm.

—. (2006) Mais além da participação pública na ciência: buscando uma reorientação dos Estudos sobre Ciência, Tecnologia e Sociedade em Ibero-américa. CTS+I. Retrieved October 28, 2015 from http://www.oei.es/revistactsi/numero7/articulo02.htm.

Deloitte and Maker Media. (2014) *Impact of the Maker Movement*. Deloitte Center for the Edge, London. Retrieved from http://www2.deloitte.com/content/dam/Deloitte/us/Documents/technology-media-telecommunications/us-maker-impact-summit2-2014-09222014.pdf.

Evangelista, R. (2011) Singularidade, transhumanismo e a ideologia da Califórnia. In *35o Encontro Anual da Anpocs*. Retrieved January 31, 2015 from http://www.anpocs.org/portal/index.php?option=com_content&view=article&id=438%3Aanais-do-encontro-mrs-gps-sps&catid=62%3A35o-encontro&Itemid=353.

Fab Foundation. (2016) "Fab Foundation – About Us". Retrieved June 2, 2016 from http://www.fabfoundation.org/about-us/.

Fonseca, F.S. (2014) Redelabs: Laboratórios Experimentais em Rede.

Fonseca, F.S. and Fleischman, L. (2014) Arranjos Experimentais Criativos em Cultura Digital. *Rede//Labs*. Retrieved March 13, 2015 from http://redelabs.org/livro/minc-14/1.

Freire, P. (1967) *Educação Como Prática da Liberdade*. Paz e Terra, Rio de Janeiro.

—. (1996) *Pedagogia da Autonomia: saberes necessários à prática educativa*. Paz e Terra, São Paulo.

Gershenfeld, N. (2012) *How to Make Almost Anything: The Digital Fabrication Revolution. Foreign Affairs 91*. Retrieved from http://cba.mit.edu/docs/papers/12.09.FA.pdf.

Gonzatto, R.F. (2014) Design de Interação e a amanualidade em Álvaro Vieira Pinto. Retrieved from http://www.utfpr.edu.br/curitiba/estrutura-universitaria/diretorias/dirppg/programas/ppgte/edital-defesas/2014/ppgte-mestrado-rodrigo-freese-gonzatto.

Hayek, F.A. (1983) *Os fundamentos da liberdade*. Editora Visão, São Paulo. Retrieved April 29, 2015 from http://www.libertarianismo.org/livros/fahofdl.pdf.

INSPER. (2016) Vestibular: Centros De Conhecimento E Laboratórios | Insper. Retrieved July 12, 2016 from http://www.insper.edu.br/vestibular/centros-de-conhecimento-e-laboratorios/

Instituto de Tecnologia Social ITS. (2016) Conheça o Fab Lab Livre SP. Retrieved May 30, 2016 from http://fablab.itsbrasil.org.br/o-que-e.

MAKER MEDIA. *Maker Media*. Retrieved July 21, 2016 from http://makermedia.com/.

Ministério do Desenvolvimento MDIC Indústria e Comércio Exterior. (2014) *Diagnostic Review of Design in Brazil*. Centro Brasil Design, Brasília. Retrieved from http://www.desenvolvimento.gov.br/arquivos/dwnl_1416924222.pdf.

Núcleo de Informática Aplicada à Educação – UNICAMP. 2000. *Super Logo 3.0*. Campinas. Retrieved from http://www.nied.unicamp.br/?q=content/super-logo-30.

Papert, S. (1997) "Why School Reform Is Impossible". *The Journal of the Learning Science*. Retrieved July 11, 2010 from http://www.papert.org/articles/school_reform.html.

—. (2008) *A máquina das crianças*. Artemed, Porto Alegre, RS.

Queluz, G.L. and Merkle, L.E. (2012) Tecnologia, Cultura e Desenvolvimento em Álvaro Vieira Pinto e Darcy Ribeiro nas décadas de 1950–60. *Espacios* 33 (1): 36–37.

Raabe, A. (2015) Espaço Maker. *Laboratório de Inovação Tecnológica na Educação (LITE)*. Retrieved February 9, 2016 from http://lite.acad.univali.br/projetos/espaco-maker/.

Sipitakiat, A., Blikstein, P., and Cavallo, D. (2004) *GoGo Board: Augmenting Programmable Bricks for Economically Challenged Audience*. In *International Conference of the Learning Sciences – Icls*. Retrieved April 12, 2015 from www.blikstein.com/paulo/documents/papers/SipitakiatBlikstein-GoGoBoard-ICLS2004.pdf.

Vieira Pinto, A. (2005) *O Conceito de Tecnologia v1*. Contraponto, Rio de Janeiro.

—. (2005) *O Conceito de Tecnologia v2*. Contraponto, Rio de Janeiro.

—. (2010) *Sete Lições sobre Educação de Adultos*. Cortez, São Paulo.

CONTRIBUTORS

Rodrigo Barbosa e Silva is a PhD Candidate at UTFPR, The Federal University of Technology - Paraná, an entrepreneur and a researcher in Brazil. He is a Systems Analyst of the Universidade Estadual do Centro-Oeste (The Midwestern State University) - UNICENTRO. Rodrigo received his Masters in Technology in 2012; currently his research aims to analyse maker movement based on Science, Technology and Society (STS), and on Brazilians authors such as Álvaro Vieira Pinto, Paulo Freire, and Paulo Blikstein. Rodrigo believes that national development, educational development and technological advances in Brazil should observe Brazilian criticisms, ideas, and envisioning to our historical process, cultures and specific characteristics of our complex society. Rodrigo has also led several robotics education initiatives. Currently he is working on software development, teaching / learning robotics, IoT and low cost open-hardware devices. In addition, Rodrigo is involved in Brazilian platforms dedicated to e-payments, body recognition, big data, natural language processing, and machine learning. Rodrigo is deeply interested in helping the national technology industry, in expanding potentials of programming and technology as a tool to emancipation, development, and freedom.

Ladan Cockshut is currently a senior lecturer in computer games at Teesside University and Junior Research Fellow at Durham University's Hatfield College. She completed her PhD in 2013 in human geography where she researched space, sociality, and competition in multiplayer game environments with her entire ethnographic research situated in the popular game World of Warcraft. Her research interests include sociality in computer and video game play, theories of play and games, crowdsourcing and games, deviance and criminality in cyberspace, innovating social science research methods, and the social policy implications of digital technologies.

Susan Just began her teaching career in government schools in Queensland and has been an educator for more than 20 years. Since then Susan has had extensive teaching and leadership experience in the independent school sector in Australia. She has been the Principal of three independent girls' schools in Queensland and Canberra, and currently Lauriston Girls' School in Melbourne. Susan holds a BA (UQ), Dip ED (UQ), M.Ed Admin (UNE), Advanced Management Course (Harvard). Susan's strong areas of interest have been in curriculum and teacher development, and this has led to her participation on a number of peak educational bodies, committees and taskforces. She has been actively involved in the Australian Heads of Independent Schools' Association, the Association of Independent Schools both in the ACT and New South Wales, the Alliance of Girls' Schools of Australasia and the Association of Australasian International Baccalaureate Schools. Susan's interest in the enhancement of STEAM in the education of young people has resulted in Lauriston Girls' School establishing the first Fablab in Australia and a working relationship with Stanford University in California.

Kenneth Y T Lim works within the intersection of cultural anthropology, the learning sciences, and cognitive psychology. He conceptualised the Six Learnings framework of curriculum design for fictive worlds and virtual environments. Most recently, his team has designed a field-based inquiry curriculum, called Maker Motes, and they are translating this approach to urban and peri-urban schools in the Association of Southeast Asian Nations (ASEAN) region. Kenneth has been a Visiting Scholar at the Hong Kong Institute of Education and was invited as a Plenary Speaker at the 2016 United Nations Educational, Scientific and Cultural Organization (UNESCO) Conference of the Asia-Pacific Programme for Educational Innovation and Development. His work has helped him posit a theory of learning around the notion of disciplinary intuitions, which he discusses in his book, Disciplinary Intuitions and the Design of Learning (2014).
Luiz Ernesto Merkle is a professor at the Federal University of Technology – at Paraná / Curitiba, Brazil; in particular at the Graduate Program on Technology and Society and at the Department of Informatics. His interests range from Science and Technology Studies, Informatics and Society, Human-Computer Interaction, to Education in Computing. He has a Ph.D. from the University of Western Ontario, and both a Masters degree and an electrical industrial engineering degree from the Federal University of Technology - at Paraná / Curitiba.

Michael Vallance is a Professor at Future University Hakodate (FUN), Japan. He has a Doctorate in Education from Durham University and a Masters Degree in Computer Assisted Learning from Stirling University, UK. He has been involved in educational technology design, implementation, research and consultancy for over fifteen years, working closely with Higher Education Institutes, schools and media companies in UK, Singapore, Malaysia and Japan. The virtual worlds research is funded by the UK Prime Minister's Initiative (PMI2) and the Japan Advanced Institute of Science and Technology (JAIST). He is also the co-founder of the International Virtual Environments Research Group (http://www.iverg.com).

INDEX